MW01145741

ORGANIZATION

—— *is a* ——

LEARNABLE SKILL

*A Memoir of How I Transformed My Life
and Reclaimed My Home in 365 Days*

By

LISA K. WOODRUFF

ISBN: 9798748906128

Past

Lessons are learned from the hard parts of our past.
I am grateful for my past struggles, reve-
lations, and experiences.

Present

Transformation is a journey that occurs
in the present, as we are rewarded
for the small changes we make each day.
I am grateful for my husband, Greg.
Thank you for supporting me and our family through
our many life transitions in the last 30 years.

Future

Rewards are the results of our transformation when
past struggles are put into perspective.
I am grateful to the younger Lisa who
had the courage to quit her job
and embrace her unique life calling.

Table of Contents

Jumping Off the Hamster Wheel

It was one of the worst days of my life.
The rain was falling hard.
The night was pitch black.
I was utterly devastated.

You've had those moments, too, haven't you? Everything was crumbling around me.

"You're not a good teacher." Those words were on a replay loop in my mind.

Those words rocked my world. The darkness and gloom around me were nothing compared to what I was feeling inside.

If I'm not a good teacher, then why am I doing this?

Striving for the approval of others…that never comes. Feeling like I let others down. Believing nothing I do is ever good enough.

"You're not a good teacher" went directly to "You're a failure" in my heart and in my mind.

This was not the first time I'd felt that way.

My mind drifted to all the other times in my life when I was told that I was not meeting expectations. I vividly remember the first time I heard that was one afternoon in sixth grade.

Twelve-year-old me bounded into my bedroom after school with my normal zeal, ready to tackle my homework. I was met by a goldenrod yellow piece of paper on my bed. I'm not sure I've cared for that shade of yellow ever since.

I could easily read the title there in black and white: "Minimum Expectations for Lisa K. Woodruff." My preteen enthusiasm dissolved in an instant. What followed was a typed list of 30 daily expectations my mother had set out for me in single-spaced text. I got to number five and stopped reading.

I was devastated. I could never in my life achieve this list even once, let alone Every. Single. Day.

My preteen-self could not reconcile an impossible list with my desire to be good and please my parents. I knew I was physically incapable of the standard of perfection set before me.

Have you been there before? Feeling like you are letting down the people you love and care about over and over again? This was my first time, but it certainly was not the last.

To this day, my mother regrets writing that list. We all make mistakes, and I've long since forgiven her. But, the truth is, I can still feel that sinking feeling.

I confess that I, too, have wanted to give my own children a similar list over the years. Just like my mom, I get frustrated when I think about what I believe my kids could and should do. My expectations of them are also unmet sometimes. What parent doesn't hold their kids up to some far-fetched and nearly impossible standards? The pain of that day has faded over the years, but the lesson has remained.

At the age of 12, I learned that I could not be perfect. And that has been truly...freeing.

Yes! Freeing! I'll let you in on a little secret—you can't be perfect, either. I know that when you read all my blog posts and listen to my podcasts, you think that I'm different, somehow. That I couldn't get into as big of a mess as you have...whether physically or emotionally. Nothing could be further from the truth. I'm going to share my journey with you, and maybe you'll catch a glimpse of yourself along the way. Remember how I said my world was crumbling? Let's start there.

I want to tell you where I started and how bad it really was. We can all learn the skills of organization, but we need to start exactly where we are, not where we think we "should" be on this journey.

Despite being a professional organizer, my own house has never been perfectly clean nor perfectly organized. (Unless you count the week we were waiting to adopt our daughter Abby…that is the only time I can remember our house not having a single to-do left undone!) I know that I'm not perfect, but I had always thrown myself into my job as a classroom teacher. That was the one area of my life that I knew I excelled.

And so the words that night from my administrator sent me into a tailspin. I was not prepared for what came next… after a long day of work and a nonsensical meeting…I just wanted to go home. What I got, instead, was what felt like a personal attack. The administrator called me in and delivered this heart-wrenching message:

"You're not a good teacher."

Define "good"?!

Teaching middle school math in a Montessori environment meant having 24 different individualized lesson plans. Every night, I stayed up until midnight preparing lessons for the next school day. Every day, I was awake by 5 a.m. in order to get my own kids off to the bus stop and myself to school on time.

If that wasn't enough, what was a "good teacher" anyway? And, who gets to decide the standard for "good"?

This time, though, I knew my administrator was wrong. I might not have a clean house or perfectly well-behaved children at home, but I was giving 110% to my job. I knew that

I *was* a good teacher. This administrator's assessment of my performance and the resulting feedback about me were both wrong. I finally got it!

Being 39 years old definitely contributed to this situation. I was *so* tired. I thought I was the only one who felt this way, overburdened with my never-ending to-do list and the mental load of trying to fill the roles of wife, mother and teacher… just to name the top three!

In the past, when I was this overwhelmed and tired, I could block off a weekend and "get my ducks in a row" and be ready to jump back in the hamster wheel on Monday morning.

But now I just felt like a depleted, tired, discouraged hamster.

So many dramatic thoughts and big emotions swirled inside me. I felt fear at not ever meeting anyone's expectations or never receiving the recognition I craved. I felt anger at once again putting everything else, including my job, above the needs of my husband and kids. Meeting my own needs didn't even figure into the mix. I was too worn out. That was probably the strongest emotion that captured my attention. I was already 39, and I realized that I had no plan for the rest of my life! All I could see was the same cycle and the same burnout, on repeat, with no end in sight. This season as a teacher was supposed to be a step up for my family, but I was definitely not reaping the benefits that my husband, Greg and I had anticipated.

In previous years, I was a stay-at-home mom. It was all I ever wanted to be. But the last seven years had been a slow and brutal slide into this present chaos.

How did I get there? How could I get out? Let's rewind a bit more. I didn't get to this point overnight.

About two years earlier, when I was 37, Greg and I were facing the largest consumer debt we had ever accumulated. I often made jokes that it was a good thing Greg and I were old, one benefit of being a Gen X-er is that we have credit from years of working! That's not actual money, mind you. Just credit.

All our lives, we had used credit to our advantage. The first time we took out a second mortgage on our house was when we adopted our son, Joey. We paid off that adoption in 14 months and then started the process again. We were blessed with the adoption of our daughter, Abby, after only two more months. There's absolutely nothing we would ever change about that part of our story. We were so happy. Fast forward to 2009 though, and we were over extended. There was nothing to do but work more, and that meant I had to go back to teaching.

I took this full-time teaching job when we were out of money and our credit was maxed out. Unfortunately, our debts kept mounting; our financial obligations and bills were growing month after month. The answer was obvious: working full-time as a teacher was only just slowing our debt accumulation, not actually reversing it. It took 18 months for us to realize this, partly because we were in survival mode and partly because it was our first time facing these life lessons.

Two months prior to my return to full-time teaching, we ended up begging the private school to readmit Joey mid-year, as the public school placement was not serving his unique needs. After three years of an amazing private educational environment that was perfectly designed for Joey's learning style and disabilities, we reluctantly chose not to renew his enrollment only because of the $20,000 tuition bill. There's nothing that feels worse than not being able to provide what you know your child needs, So, we kept pushing, with both of us working full-time and neither of us being able to see the real damage unfolding before us.

Isn't that what happens? You push so hard, and it takes a crisis to change your course. I knew I was working beyond my capacity, but I'd always been able to just keep going.

Riding the roller coaster of the economy, the bankruptcy of the direct sales company I represented, my parents' separation and divorce, and my father's illness and then death were becoming too much to handle. I wanted off the hamster wheel. What could we do to make this stop? I had always juggled too much. Changing that broken system felt so foreign, but it had to happen.

Back to that hurtful day in December 2011, being told that I basically was a failure by someone whose opinion about my performance was supposed to matter. Remember the rain?

Remember the darkness? Conditions were as bad as they could be… but yet perfect for what had to happen next. As I drove home from that ill-fated meeting and away from those despised words from my administrator, I kept running the numbers in my head and coming to the same conclusion. There wasn't enough money—no matter what I did.

Failure? I did not accept failure. I didn't then, and I don't now. There is always another way. I had been focusing all of my energy on being the best teacher I could. That night, I was told my best was not good enough. Those words will put a hard pause in the middle of anyone's week, but they were life-changing for me. I woke up during that drive home—to a difficult realization.

All of my waking hours were devoted to a job that was not earning as much as we needed. I felt like I was failing on all fronts.

I. Was. A. Failure.

Five years of trying harder, sleeping less, and putting everyone else first had failed.

My 40th birthday was just around the corner, and I could not accept this as my lot in life. When I was a child, I had two dreams. One dream was to be a wife and mother. The second dream was to own my own business and be an entrepreneur just like my mother, grandmother, great-grandmother, father, and grandfather. It was in my genes and in my blood.

I could accept my failure as a teacher, but I would never forgive myself if I failed my family. I knew that only I could be a wife to Greg and a mother to Joey and Abby. They were and always will be my first and most important priority.

When I remembered my second dream, I started to realize that I did have a way out. I come from a long line of hard-working people who just made it happen–whatever business they were in–because they had to. I had to make it happen, too. This was my time to join the family legacy of doing whatever it takes.

I had dabbled in a few side hustles in the past, but this was different. I knew it was time to get off of the hamster wheel. It was my time to quit my job, come home, and start my own business. At first, I had no idea what that business would be, but I knew I could do something. Anything was better than the path I was on now.

I pulled in the driveway, walked in the door, and told my husband that I was going to quit my teaching job. That's just how I am. No nonsense…direct…matter-of-fact.

"Fine," he said, keeping his eyes glued to the game on TV. No questions. No comment besides, "Fine."

"I really am!" I called back as I turned to go upstairs.

"Ok!" he acknowledged as though I'd just told him it was time for dinner. Maybe the clouds and darkness from my drive had clung to me, and he didn't want to know more until after I'd settled. Or, maybe he knew the signs of when I had made a decision and knew to stay out of my way. We're a great team that way.

I started up the stairs. I stopped at each of the kids' bedrooms, checking to see that they had what they needed to get their work done before school tomorrow. Being the last day of the school year before winter break, no homework was due and the kids were in a favorable mood.

I got settled on my bed, opened my laptop and started to write.

An hour later, I had finished my resignation letter, and I walked back downstairs to have my husband read it.

I stood there as he read, making sure he really did know the full extent of what I was doing. Throughout our 25 years of marriage, Greg has never told me "no" or stopped me from anything I felt convicted to do. But this was big. Huge. I was giving up a consistent paycheck for…what?!

I didn't know what my next step was at the time. I knew this was the answer, but I couldn't see how the math was going to work. It didn't work with what I was currently doing, but I couldn't really see a clear path forward, either. I just knew that changing my course was the only option.

"Do it," Greg said, snapping me out of my thoughts.

"Are you sure?" I replied, suddenly a little less certain of those passionate convictions of only a few moments before.

"Yes," he said, handing me the letter and turning his attention back to the TV. The decision was made. We were in this together…whatever *this* was. We would step off the hamster wheel and face the future together.

The next morning was the Friday before winter break. I arrived at school early, slipped my resignation letter under my administrator's locked door, and made my way to my classroom to let my co-teacher know I was done teaching. I was finished teaching in *that* classroom and at *that* school. I had yet to find *my* classroom. The classroom where I was uniquely created to teach. The classroom where I could share the most compelling lessons I'd ever have the privilege to teach.

From Overwhelm to a Plan

It was mid-January 2012 by the time my teaching replacement was found, and I was free to leave my job. Somehow, I thought that simply returning home would magically transport me back 7 years in time to when I was in control of my schedule, our finances, and our home.

It did not.

I took the kids to school and settled into my new role. My first task as a newly-returned-home homemaker was to go to the grocery store. I proceeded to do as I had always done, shopping early at my favorite grocery store, Meijer. If you are not from the Midwest, perhaps you have never heard of the chain, but trust me…it's worth a trip.

The reason I love Meijer is because you can literally buy anything there. I detest having to get in and out of my car, so having one store where you can "get it all" is my dream come true.

I wandered up and down every single aisle, filing 2 carts with the "necessities" I *knew* we needed. I love a fresh start, and shopping is one way we can seek to create that feeling.

I arrived home at 10 a.m. and started unloading the car.

It is amazing to me how much we live our lives based on past actions and scripts that we write for ourselves. Driving home, I already saw the errors of my ways. We were in debt and I had no job, yet my first action was to "fill the cart." Oh, we "fill the carts" in our lives for many reasons. I'm sure that I was both soothing myself with the shopping and trying to instantly fall back into the "role" of a stay-at-home mom. So, naturally, my first instinct was to run away from home and to the store.

After unloading the car, I opened the kitchen cabinets and the refrigerator to put away my bounty and realized that they were all full. I looked around my grocery bag-laden kitchen and realized this problem was bigger than the hours spent at a job away from home. I realized that I had no idea what items we already owned. It was like I was standing in a friend's kitchen and she was asking me for help. I was seeing my kitchen with different eyes, as though for the first time.

How did it get this bad? When did I lose control?

I took a few bags of bathroom supplies upstairs and found similar overstuffed, disorganized closets and cabinets there.

I slowly walked back downstairs to the kitchen in disbelief. I didn't recognize my own home. I had spent months blindly sleepwalking through my life. I knew something needed to change, and I knew it had to start with me.

I do my best thinking with a legal pad and Flair felt-tip pens. Always a teacher, I sat at the kitchen table and tried to reconcile the totality of the situation. My brain went immediately into action.

The first thing to do is make a plan. Plan? I can do that. I'm an expert planner. I've got this.

This moment was about way more than finding a home for my over-purchased cereal bars and toothpaste tubes. I needed to write down a plan so I wouldn't unnecessarily start filling my time and my schedule (as well as my cupboards) and find myself somewhere down this new path without the real change I knew our family needed.

I had 3 competing priorities:

1. I needed to reassert myself in my children's education and advocate for their futures.
2. I needed to replace and then surpass my teaching salary.
3. I needed to reclaim my home.

I had no worries about tackling my role in my children's education and advocating for their futures. That was and always will be my main priority, the reason I get up every morning and my last thought of every day. That left me with two remaining priorities. I was determined to gain control and figure out how to get all three of these things done.

Logically, earning an income should have taken priority, but, realistically, I knew the house had to come first. Every teacher knows—you have to get your classroom in order before you do anything else. But, I had to think bigger. The house was just the beginning.

I instinctively started my list with getting my home organized. Years later, I know that this was the best possible first step. Over many years as a professional organizer, I have seen how a disorganized home can keep a person trapped and prevent them from achieving their unique purpose on this planet.

Your house will likely be *your* first step, too. I can't wait until you see how much more time and freedom you have when your home is decluttered and organized. I have heard from lots of people who have transformed their lives by first getting their homes organized. Your day is coming, and I can't wait to see what you have to offer the world!

I knew I needed a system for addressing the chaos in my home. What was my plan going to be?

Obviously, my little shopping trip proved that what worked in the past would not work now. It was time for something new.

I needed an actionable checklist in order to map out the whole project and then organize it into bite-sized chunks. I used my teaching skills and made myself a lesson plan for resetting my home. I hadn't yet realized it, but organization is a *learnable* skill, one that *anyone* can learn.

I made a list of 40 distinct spaces in my home that needed to be decluttered and organized. I used this list as the focus of my initial posts for the Organize 365 blog I had just started.

More happened that day at the kitchen table than meets the eye. Yes, I made a list of spaces to declutter and organize. Yes, I took control. But, the biggest thing that happened that day was that I took back ownership of my household. I made the most important change of all: I changed my mindset.

Win or lose, I was going to be in control of my space again. I was invested in and committed to being the keeper of my home. The ones who would benefit most would be the ones who most needed my attention. My days were no longer going to be focused on everyone else living outside those four walls. I was clear about what I was doing and who I would be doing it for as I started out on this new journey.

With that kind of motivation, there was no possibility of failure. I knew it wouldn't be perfect. In fact, it was much harder than I thought to make that shift a reality, but that morning I committed to changing my trajectory in life. I was in control. I was responsible for the outcome, and I was done living a reactive life.

Organization Project #1: The Kitchen

As I set out to reclaim my home, I started in the kitchen. It took me seven long days at the end of January to get my kitchen back in shape. I was surprised at how long it really took to organize that space. But doesn't it make sense? The kitchen is the heart of most homes, and mine was no different. Most of our real living takes place in and around the kitchen, so that space is at the core of lasting success.

Day 1–Food–it's complicated

I tackled all the food spaces first. The pantry, the refrigerator, and the freezer all got a thorough cleaning. This first step proved to be so painful.

I had multiple trash bags full of expired food. It made me sick to look at the waste of resources and money I was literally throwing down the drain. I was out of a job and throwing out food? It felt unbelievably wasteful and frustrating, but I also knew keeping expired food would not feed my family or bring back the money I had spent. I had to give myself permission to let go of the bad choices and out of control spending that were holding me back from the organized future that I craved. I knew that I was going for a greater goal and had to stay focused.

My relationship with food would be best explained as… "it's complicated." There are so many emotions tied to food for me, and I bet you can relate. I love sweets, appetizers, desserts, and snack foods, none of which are particularly healthy or full of nutrients. I can eat the same meals over and over and over, so I don't require or desire a lot of variety. I have no problem getting vitamins and nutrition in supplements so that I can enjoy my sweets.

Not great… I know. Some of you may be cringing, but I want to be honest. This is who I am. Cleaning out my freezer was in itself a trip down memory lane.

My mom was very familiar with the Stouffer's brand of frozen foods founded in her hometown of Cleveland, Ohio. So, throughout my childhood, that same goodness found its way to our family's freezer…and into my heart. Have you ever had Stouffer's lasagna? Oh, my! Why would you ever go to the work to make that dish from scratch when Stouffer's does such a good job!? And everybody knows that your childhood tastes can have a huge influence on what you prefer as an adult. I love Stouffer's.

My mother was an entrepreneur and started a company in our basement when I was in fourth grade. Her creating strengths were in crafting and entrepreneuring—not cooking.

Most nights while mom worked, my sister and I would consult the freezer and pick any Stouffer's meal or TV dinner we wanted. A few times a week, we would have a simple family dinner of meat, potatoes, bread, and corn. I didn't realize it as a child, but by focusing on her strengths, my mom was teaching me how to decide what I cared about and how to foster those gifts. She helped me to learn to give myself grace for not meeting some imaginary standard by cooking the perfect lasagna from scratch when I would rather be focusing on my family and gaining control of my home.

Like my mother, the business and craft ideas in my head always kept me more entertained than planning and executing an evening dinner. However, in 2005, after 10 years of marriage and with 2 small children underfoot, I turned my creative, researching brain toward the nutrition (or lack thereof) in our diets.

Even as preschoolers, both of my kiddos had sensory issues, allergic tendencies, and some behavior struggles. After much reluctance, I decided to try modifying their diets. Despite being the queen of the freezer meal, I was going to try to cook!

As luck would have it, both kids got the stomach flu at the same time when they were 3 and 4 years old. After 3 days of Gatorade and not much else, they started to feel better. I capitalized on this bout of the flu as the starting point of an elimination diet. With no food in their systems, I could easily see how each ingredient affected their health. Gone were the days of conveniently ignoring those long package labels. I would know the ingredients of everything our family ate because I was going to be the one to make it.

Joey's reactions were easy to see and understand. We gave Joey straight cow's milk, and instantly he began climbing everything in sight and had an angry energy. He repeatedly bit his toys and blanket. A few hours later, we tried Triscuits. Triscuits only have the following ingredients: whole wheat, salt and oil. Within minutes, Joey was wheezing. Frustratingly, Abby's reactions were not as easy to observe as Joey's were, but she definitely had reactions to common foods, as well.

I shudder to recall those early days of food testing with my kids. There is nothing more terrifying than seeing your child have an allergic reaction–unless it is thinking, "What am I going to feed these people?!" I would need to be vigilant about every single ingredient they ate.

Neither of my kids have tested allergic to any foods, despite their obvious reactions. Over the next few years, I would identify many foods and additives that caused health and behavioral changes in them both, in spite of what the sophisticated medical tests were supposed to rule out. I believe that every mom is the *expert* about her children (and I believe the same for you dads out there, too!). I was interested in trying *every possible* non-medical alternative that might help me gain control while helping my kids grow, thrive and eventually succeed at life.

Two years later, with Abby and Joey at the ages of five and six, I did the unthinkable. I moved my kids to a completely gluten-free and casein-free diet. In case you don't understand the significance of this, that means that all foods containing grain and dairy (grain and dairy!) were out of their lives. For 18 months, any morsel the kids ate I made from scratch at home. Abby's reactions were more severe, so she had the most restrictive diet of the two. God bless you warrior mamas (and dads!) with me on the road to do anything possible to make your child's life better.

For us, this new diet wasn't just a gluten-free version of macaroni and cheese. Oh no, we eliminated over 35 ingredients from our diet including eggs, soy, potato, most oils and so much more. The kids still talk about how I made fake goldfish crackers and cooked with duck eggs. They survived—we all did—but those memories are from a crisis time in our lives. Who has time to do anything else when planning and cooking three meals a day every single day?

Joey's diet was not as strict as Abby's, but going gluten and casein-free in 2005 was not as easy as it is today. I had millet bread flown in from Florida and nitrate-free hotdogs flown in from Pennsylvania. I spent our whole paycheck at Whole Foods and over 40 hours a week in our kitchen creating quasi-edible meals. I was longing for my old friend, Stouffer's, but I knew I had to do this for our family.

The body is an amazing creation. After 18 months of this level of attention, most of our kids' food sensitivities were resolved and their guts had finally healed. I'm so grateful that the kids were eventually able to resume more typical diets, but those 18 months were a marathon. Honestly, the financial cost and time spent were unsustainable, and our kids' compliance was waning. It was time to move back to a more normal eating routine.

Unfortunately, I had completely burned myself out in the kitchen department. That, plus the other onslaughts that came into our lives in the years between 2005 and 2011, diverted my energy and attention from our typical food preparation routine to a season when we were eating for sustenance only. Our family's kitchen has seen it all, and there is more than food stored in those cabinets. There are memories, associations, guilty pleasures, and more than one nightmare lingering there, too.

And that is why I struggled so much on day one in my kitchen. It wasn't just the food I was decluttering. It was the failed attempts to provide perfect nutrition for my family, the dream of the fabulous home chef I have never been, and the lack of desire to apply myself to change that. Each thing I threw out was a reminder of how my life wasn't exactly like I believed it would or should be.

I never have changed to become a mom who spends a lot of time preparing family meals. I have a lot of strengths. Cooking, meal planning, and making a family dinner are not on the list. I am still working on accepting my imperfect food habits and priorities. Stouffer's is still in business for a reason! I am not the only one who has different priorities than home cooking. I have never apologized for doing what I thought was right for myself and my family. I want you to find this freedom, too. It starts by letting go of what no longer serves you or your family.

It was a struggle, but I decluttered the expired food and regained an ounce of control. I determined that the food spaces in my kitchen looked good. Day 1 complete.

Day 2–"Just in case" cooking supplies

The next day, I moved on to dishes, pots, pans, and all other cooking-related supplies. Oh, if you could have seen the contraptions I still had from those cooking science experiment days! Pressure cookers, juicers, a ladle for homemade gluten-free bagels, and even two toasters–one for gluten bread and one for gluten-free bread! The list went on and on.

On the first try, I did not declutter it all. It was all *so* expensive, and nobody likes to throw out the "investments" that we make, even if they are no longer useful to us. I did move some to the basement so they were out of sight, but those devices were still there "just in case."

Just in case.
Just in case we do the gluten-free, casein-free diet again?
Just in case I decide to be a regular cook and bake from scratch?
Just in case I *need* it for…
For what? What was I going to need it for?

As I decluttered and organized, I observed my thoughts as I processed each item. So. Many. Thoughts.

One simple item, a pressure cooker, elicited all these thoughts. Why did I buy this? I wish I had that $100 back. I shouldn't have spent my money so carelessly. Pressure cookers make me so nervous. I am afraid it will explode! But, Greg loves artichokes. How else would I make artichokes? And why do only 2 artichokes fit in here? How am I supposed to make 4 for our family? Maybe there is a bigger pressure cooker? (Goes to Google.) What am I doing? I don't have money for a bigger pressure cooker; I don't even use this one!

Next, I picked up our apple peeler corer slicer from Pampered Chef. (Side note–I love Pampered Chef products. The evidence of my love was all over the kitchen. I had *all* kinds of Pampered Chef gadgets.) As a preschool teacher, I used the apple peeler corer slicer at school. The kids loved it, and we made various apple treats. However, at home it was bulky, messy, took up a lot of space, and I never used it. Will I ever make a homemade apple pie? What about apple strudel? Even if I do make it, how long would it take us to eat it? We shouldn't be eating that way anyway!

Wading through these feelings of guilt about getting rid of perfectly good items I had spent our hard-earned money on was exhausting. Plus, I was wrestling with letting go of my dreams of being the kind of mom who made artichokes and apple pies (and had kids who would eat them!). At the end of the day, my brain was tired, and I hadn't even gone anywhere.

Despite those awful, heavy feelings, I was determined to make our kitchen a space for our family–the actual family we have today. I thought about what I would say to a friend beating herself up for being human and having made some bad decisions. Guilt, shame, regret, and stress were not going to bring back the money. I began to explore giving myself grace. I stopped beating myself up for what was done and focused on what I needed to do now. I put the gadgets into the donation box and began to reclaim my kitchen and regain control of our home.

The physical release of moving the donations to the car, and "just in case items" to the basement definitely made me feel better–like a weight had been lifted. I had been lifting both physical and emotional weights all day, and the progress was already showing.

Day 3–One kitchen drawer at a time

By now, I was in deep. You know the feeling when you have started something, but you are not sure how to accomplish the task or if you are even capable of doing so? That is where I was on Day 3. I was too far in to pretend I didn't have a goal, but not quite sure how it would all get done. I was working furiously all day while the kids were in school. My other household responsibilities were met with what I would later call "planned neglect." I wasn't doing other things like vacuuming, dusting or laundering my sheets. I made a decision to prioritize what *most* needed my focus right now and to put all of my available time and energy into that.

Fortunately for me, Greg has gotten used to my "projects." For the most part, he rolls with whatever passion project I have undertaken. Getting our house under control was my number one project. I was still following the lesson plan I had developed for organizing the house, and I was making progress.

In the future, I would modify this household clean-up challenge into a more manageable 100 Day Home Organization Program. On that day though, I was a woman with a mission. I just hoped my determination could hold out until I saw more results. Haven't we all started with a bang and ended with a whimper? Making progress each day helped me to stay motivated and keep going.

Giving myself seven days of my plan for the kitchen alone was genius. The kitchen is a monster organizing task with emotional pitfalls at every turn. In the past, I would have worked this room in clockwise fashion, organizing each space top to bottom. But, this time I didn't do that. This time, I divided the kitchen into zones of use and tackled those objectives no matter where the items were stored. Kitchen zones are specific to how you use your kitchen, but some common ones including baking supplies, everyday dishes, drinkware, food storage containers, canned goods and so on.

Getting through all the food and cooking items in the first two days gave me a good start. Next, I tackled all the drawers. Do your kitchen drawers and cabinets hold memories? Mine sure do.

My grandfather on my father's side built a house for his family of five children in 1962. This beautiful home in Rocky River,

Ohio, had two great big bedrooms connected with a bathroom across the front of the house. This space was for my dad's four sisters, two in each room. My father had a single bedroom in the back that he soon shared with a new baby brother, 14 years his junior.

My father was just 23 when I was born. As the oldest grandchild, I spent quite a bit of time at my grandparents' house. Having a photographic memory, I can visually see and easily remember my grandmother preparing meals for our large family, and I can recall the constant snacking that happened there, too.

I was especially intrigued by the cabinet that opened on the kitchen table side of the counter, for it held a treasure…boxes of cereal! My aunts and uncles would pack themselves 3 and 4 to a bench and slide into the table requesting cereal boxes that could be grabbed while still seated. I loved this introduction to functional organization! Homes should be used for the people who live in them, not for some magazine-worthy publication.

After my father passed away in 2009, I used part of my inheritance to remodel our kitchen. Even though we were in debt at the time, I am still happy we made that investment. Our kitchen has #allthestorage. Top on my renovation list was more drawers. You can never have too many drawers!

Our original kitchen had the standard configuration of a single drawer on top with a cabinet below it. But I wanted more drawers! And if I were to do my kitchen over again, I might put in ALL drawers. Did I mention that I love drawers?

On the kitchen table side of our cabinets, I added a set of four drawers just like I saw in my grandparents' home. I used these drawers for the kids' school and art supplies for many years. Inside the kitchen, I had a bank of four drawers for silverware and kitchen tools as well as plastic bags and wraps. Nobody ever has designated space for these items, but I did! I knew what I needed to regain control of our home, and, for us, that even included a bread drawer!

I am far from a minimalist; however, the idea of an empty counter does appeal to me. As I was cleaning out my drawers from leftover baby items and tools I would never use, I wondered what if I could get the utensils currently on display in my countertop crock into a drawer instead?

I knew to do so, I would have to do two things. First, I would have to declutter more so that the utensils would fit. That I knew I could do. The harder step would be to convince my husband that his precious kitchen utensils did not need to be on the counter. A man and his tools are hard to part, and this would be putting them out of sight. For me, that would be perfect. For him, though? I thought I would have to do some convincing.

Today, my husband does all the cooking. (*Cue the angels singing.*) Back then, I was still the person pretending to cook.

Greg's mom is an amazing cook. Amazing. She and everyone else I know who are good cooks have a crock of utensils on their counter. As they should. They use them.

But, the truth is, we did not use ours. We used two or three items out of the 20 in the crock. And the ones we did use were used only a few times a week. In my opinion, that was not frequently enough to justify keeping a whole crock on the counter every day.

It was day three, and I was on a roll, so I did it. I got rid of the utensil crock. Why not? What did I have to lose?

Greg came home and immediately asked, "Where is the utensil crock?"

I explained my reasoning, and he didn't seem convinced, but I didn't put it back, either.

I relocated the crock to the basement "just in case" pile and told him we could always bring it back. "Let's just try this" was all I said. Little did I know what an impact those clear, clean counters would have on our family and on so many families worldwide. I still love the feeling I get when I enter my kitchen to those glistening and empty flat surfaces. Trust me…you will, too!

Day 4–Cabinets are mini rooms

Cabinets were next on my agenda for the week. I like to view cabinets like small rooms. This may be an unusual perspective, but hear me out. The fact that you have to open a door to access what you need is akin to opening a door to a room. As such, each cabinet needs a purpose. My problem was I had way too many purposes and not enough cabinets!

I did the unthinkable and completely emptied out ALL the cabinets at one time. It was complete chaos. Don't do it.

I quickly replaced all the dishes back in the dishes cabinet. And, luckily, I hadn't emptied the spice cabinet yet, because adding spices to that chaotic mess might have forced me to call it a day. I saved that for later. I was left with an obscene number of reusable plastic storage containers, lunch boxes, mugs, water bottles, drinking glasses, blenders, vases, baking supplies, serving dishes, wine glasses, casserole dishes, bread pans, holiday serving pieces, and more. I had no idea that so much clutter had been lurking behind those innocent-looking cabinet doors. How often did I use this stuff…any of it? What really deserved that much square footage? I was about to find out.

I asked myself a few key questions to see if I could get a better organization solution than the one I had in place.

1. If I were just moving into my house today, how would I arrange these items into little rooms?

2. How does my family use these items? Do we even use most of them?

3. What items do I use on a regular basis? I knew there were some, and they needed to occupy that valuable real estate.

Greg and I moved into our home on our one year wedding anniversary. It was and still is perfect for our family. As I mentioned earlier, one of my major life goals was to be a wife and mom. When we were house hunting, I wanted to be sure I had a space where the babies could be corralled when they were little and could play in my line of sight when they got a bit older. I also *love* to take a bubble bath at night, so I knew a soaking tub was on my must-have list for my dream home.

Somehow, in the bustle of everyday life, 14 years and two soon-to-be middle school-aged kids later, I had not changed anything about how we used our kitchen. As much as I used to dream about my future, I forgot to look around as my kids grew and changed to see what they needed in different phases of their childhood. As I puzzled through the questions running through my head, a few nontraditional thoughts came to mind:

1. I wanted to create more "pre-adult self-serve areas" to help Abby and Joey learn some valuable skills and feel welcome in this central area of our home.

2. I don't like to cook dinner, but I do like to bake treats.

3. I like to entertain or bring a dessert over on the holidays on thematic serving dishes. I especially like thematic holiday

cookie trays. For me, it was important to have a place to store these because I enjoy them. They are important to me.

While thinking about my cabinets like little rooms, I divided my piles into some general categories. I had supplies for lunches, baking, holiday-themed items, drinks of all types and serving pieces. I moved all seasonal and holiday pieces into the basement with the appropriate seasonal bins. (Ok, Ok. I didn't have an organized bin area yet, but I did have a holiday corner. I added them there. See, I'm definitely not perfect, but I *do* celebrate my progress.) I saved baking and lunch items for another day and put the rest back where they had been before the kitchen had exploded, knowing that I wasn't done with the cabinet yet and would address them again tomorrow.

Day 5–When in doubt, sleep on it

As often happens, I had a great idea as I slept on the night before day five. My favorite version of multitasking is to have my brain puzzle through an issue in the middle of the night. I awoke full of energy and ready to tackle the kitchen once again. I had the answer I was looking for, just by letting my brain work while I slept. Day five was going to be great!

For both preschool and kindergarten, Joey and Abby attended the Montessori school where I had taught. I love the Montessori approach and philosophy of education and empowerment. In a truly devoted teacher fashion, our home mirrored that Montessori environment when our kids were younger. Our playroom looked like a classroom, and our pantry had two shelves specifically set aside so that the kids could help themselves to snacks independently.

When we remodeled our kitchen in 2009, the kids were no longer in Montessori school, and our pantry was replaced with a long counter and pantry cabinets. We designed a kitchen with some intentional modifications to the layout so that it would better fit the needs of our family for that stage of our lives.

Our former kitchen had a planning desk and pantry with a door on one wall. The wall was nine feet long! I was picturing future holiday gatherings, graduation parties, and adult children when I had all of that replaced with a nine foot long countertop with pantry cabinets below. It was quite a different configuration, and initially I didn't realize I had taken away the kids' "self-serve" area in the process. To be fair, by now the kids could reach most of what the adults could, so I didn't think a designated area was necessary, but my middle-of-the-night brain disagreed.

That morning as I was packing lunches, I observed that what my brain had told me was true. To get a lunch packed in our kitchen, you had to open almost every cabinet and drawer. It was completely inefficient. Here are the items I collected on my "open and close" the door activity.

- Lunch boxes
- Water bottles
- Reusable plastic tubs & lids

- Plastic bags
- Plastic silverware
- Chips
- Fruit cups
- All the sandwich fixings
- Desserts
- Juice boxes

After I returned from school drop off, I looked again at the space and thought about the process we went through every single weekday during the school year. If each cabinet was functioning as a small room, why was I keeping each lunch item in a different room? How could I get almost all of those items in one location? First, I realized that the chips, fruit cups and desserts were being stored with other snack food items, but the intent was that they would only be used for lunches. I pulled all of those out and put them together. While I was at it, I pulled out all the breakfast items as well. Those were also scattered in multiple cabinets and were actually needed only in the mornings.

Once the food items were on the counter, I decided to go all in, pulling lunch boxes and bags, plastic forks & spoons, water bottles and more out of every cabinet. It took quite a bit of puzzling and cabinet swapping to make the new breakfast and lunch packing cabinet come into being. But it was worth it! I kept reopening the new breakfast/lunch cabinet and marveling at the organization.

You think I'm joking, but you will understand when you find yourself giddy about an area that you finally organized and feel like is truly functional for your daily life! At the end of the day, I felt like I was not only getting organized, I was actually starting to put into place new systems that would save me time going forward.

Day 6–Done is better than perfect

I had budgeted two more kitchen organizing days in my plan. On day six, I decided I would focus on spices and recipes. For someone who doesn't cook from scratch, I sure found a lot of prime real estate being taken up by little bottles and jars. We had a *lot* of spices. I tossed the expired ones and cleaned out the rest of my two skinny cabinets that house oils, spices and baking supplies.

Spices were fun to declutter and organize; however, the project I was dreading was the recipes. Just like with the lunch supplies, somehow our recipes were spread out in multiple cabinets.

Like Greg's mother, my grandma was a fantastic cook. As a gift for my wedding, she wrote out all of her recipes onto cards just for me. My grandmother had the tiniest, most elegant handwriting. Seeing those recipes written out with so much love still makes me smile.

I had a wooden recipe box that housed all my grandmother's recipes, as well as those I had saved over the years on recipe cards. I also had printed recipes from the computer and those torn out of magazines. Most of those magazine recipes were folded into the recipe box, as well. A smattering of traditional cookbooks, cooking magazines, and appliance cookbooks added to the collection. In the future, I wanted to have all my recipes in one streamlined system. I finally had them all in one location! That would have to do at this point.

Perfectionism is not something you can quit cold-turkey. It comes back in sneaky ways. It is; however, a mindset that you can change by recognizing it and learning to focus on new thought patterns. As I was coming to the end of my week in the kitchen, my list of what I could do better grew. I was still tempted by a vision of a "perfect" kitchen in a "perfectly organized" home, but I was beginning to realize I would never be truly done organizing if my goal was perfection. I came to the conclusion that this week's work was good enough, and I wanted to focus on recognizing and celebrating my progress.

Day 7–Starting to see progress!

The next morning, I was reenergized! A smile unconsciously spread across my face as I opened the newly organized cabinets, drawers and specifically defined spaces for kids, cookbooks and baking. I was starting to see and feel the progress, and it felt amazing! By the end of the week, I had decluttered about 40% of the items in my kitchen.

I finished the rest of the room that day by taking everything off the kitchen counters and giving them a good scrub. I returned only the knife block, tv, fruit bowl, and coffee maker back to their places on the countertops. I was excited, empowered, and deeply satisfied in a job well done. Despite my success, I couldn't help but think, "how did this get so bad?!" and more importantly, "how can I prevent it from happening again?"

I was one week into this new journey, but yet I knew that I had a lifetime to go in order to make it really work. I wanted real change and nothing was going to stop me! But to move forward, I had to dive into what really got me into this situation. I knew what kind of stress caused this mess, but how would I keep it from creeping back into my life?

I initially documented these seven days as blog posts on the old *organize365.com* website as part of the The 40 Days ~ One Whole House Challenge. Those first entries are no longer accessible online. I realized that the spaces in your home were too broad and the program was hyper focused to help 40-year-old stay-at-home moms with preteens. I wanted my experience to be a benefit for all of you coming behind me. I wanted a more effective home organization lesson plan to guide you in transforming your own home.

Today, Organize 365 offers a more streamlined and functional program which covers all the main areas of your home that need to be organized. I designed the 100 Day Program for *any* adult living in *any* size house, *anywhere* in the world. The 100 tasks can be done in as little as 15 minutes a day (although you may want to spend 30-45 minutes on some days of your first round). I used my Montessori background to guide you through organizing your home three times in a calendar year. The Montessori model works for adult learning, too! Remember, progress over perfection. It can be done!

We've walked through the first seven days of my journey. Now, let's explore the rest of my house and the rest of my year as I transformed and developed my organization skills. I had made a plan, completed the scheduled tasks, and now all I had to do was just keep swimming!

Learning to Take Action

I looked at my schedule and carved out 20 days to work on my home during the month of February. I was poised to be 75% of the way done with my organizing project by March 1st! After the kitchen, I felt unstoppable! The living room, dining room, and family rooms were all going to be a breeze. They were part of my original plan, but more importantly, they were part of maintaining my feeling of success. I found that once I had such a large area organized, my motivation to gain control of the rest of my house was through the roof! As I reflect back on the winter of 2012, I can still feel the sheer determination that pushed me to succeed at reclaiming my home. I wanted to earn the trust that Greg had put in my ability to regain control of our lives after quitting my job.

In February, my days were spent creating the Organize 365 blog, building my presence in a new direct sales business, cleaning other people's homes, going to doctor appointments, and attending school meetings for my kids. I was busy, but I was motivated! I was focusing on being a wife and a mother while also trying to earn some sort of income for our family. I continued on my journey to transform our home.

Each evening, after school pick up, homework, and dinner were all completed for the day, I would tackle the next space on my list. The week I gave myself in January to work on the kitchen while the kids were at school definitely gave me a jumpstart; now, I needed to learn how to fit my organizational sprints in around my other obligations and family responsibilities.

My three priorities for the month were to reestablish my Sunday Basket® routine, meet my income earning goal, and declutter and organize our home.

The Sunday Basket®

When I opened my eyes to the disaster that our house had become, I easily created a list of spaces in my home that needed my attention. I had been here before; the feelings of disorganization and lack of control were all too familiar. In 2002, when Abby was 6 months and Joey was 2 years old, I just couldn't keep it all together. I had lost control of my home organization back then, too. Ironically, the two episodes of disorganization happened for opposite reasons—lack of time and lack of income.

In 2002, we were earning more money than we ever had. We had zero debt, and my direct sales business was booming. My problem was that I didn't have enough *time*, and when I did have time, I didn't know where to start! Sound familiar?! I had so many papers that needed my attention, and my extensive to-do lists were everywhere.

It was a random Sunday night, and I was determined to regain control. I separated out the papers that required action from the rest of the stack. I laid out all of my actionable to-do papers into 40 different piles according to topic...errands, bills, school, medical, etc. Then, I put each pile into an individual plastic slash pocket and corralled them in a basket that I happened to have in the same room. Each Sunday, I would take the time to sort through my papers again and plan my "must-dos" for the week. And that, my friends, is how The Sunday Basket® was born!

The beauty of the Sunday Basket® was–that it worked! The next day at nap time, I grabbed a single slash pocket, did the to-dos, and moved on. (*Cue the singing angels again!*) For an exhausted 30-year-old mother of two kids under two, getting anything accomplished and checked off my list was a praise-worthy event.

Over the years, I had waxed and waned in my Sunday Basket® habit. Habits are funny like that. When you first establish new habits, you see what a miracle they can be in your life. You appreciate how they save so much time and reduce decision fatigue. Then life gets in the way and you skip a week here and there. The next thing you know, you are back where you started, and you can't figure out how you got there.

While I did get a lot done in January, there were also days where I lost time…90 minutes driving something to school that we forgot, an appointment I left off my calendar and missed, and even more reactive moments that cost me both time and money.

As I worked on the habit of processing my Sunday Basket® each and every week, I began to find that planning saved me time. I began to make proactive decisions rather than be pulled in so many different directions as I encountered whatever came my way. I was able to make a list of errands and get them all done on the same day! (I just heard you gasp. Don't deny it. I know, it *does* seem too good to be true!) I created a list of phone calls to make and had all the necessary paperwork readily available when I sat down with my phone. I looked ahead and planned for transportation for the kids to school or activities. Most importantly, I was able to get organized enough to free up some time to work on my business to help it grow.

Past Successes Are Seeds to New Breakthroughs.

Ok, back to 2012. We were up to our eyeballs in debt; I was doing everything I could think of to figure out how to earn more money for our family. In addition to cleaning houses and running my direct sales businesses, I focused on growing the audience of my blog. I knew that I could earn an income through the blog, but I needed to have something to sell. I had already written the ebook, *How to Organize the Business of Direct Sales* (no longer available), which I sold at speaking engagements. Ebook bundles were extremely popular in 2012. I wanted to get a new ebook published quickly in order to make a profit and gain visibility for the Organize 365 blog.

Although I had been in the blogging world since 2009, my time and effort had not yet brought in a profit. I had a small blog in 2009-2010, but I had decided to pursue teaching instead of developing an online brand at that time. Even so, I continued attending the meetings of my local blogging community to learn about the possibilities for my future in that area. I listened to the speakers and watched what was going on in the industry as website views and monetization changed from Google ad revenue, to coupon printing commissions, to huge Facebook page audiences, and then on to ebook bundles.

I dusted off my own Sunday Basket® process for myself and began writing. By the end of the month, I had my ebook written and ready to go in the April Homemaking Bundle. I wasn't sure exactly how much I might earn, but it was a start. "Lisa Math" is a real thing, especially when it comes to earning money. As a big picture visionary, I often miss the details. I can underestimate how long an organizing project will take and how much things will cost, while I overestimate my energy to get it all done. My team is often overwhelmed by my audacious goal setting.

As I have aged, I am finally realizing that what I could physically accomplish in my 20's is not a reality in my late 40's. In spite of what I may now lack in physical stamina, I have gained in mental capacity. I like to say that most days, my brain and mouth are the parts of me that get the most exercise!

I don't see many problems as an "either/or" scenario. I can always see options, and I like to create new paths and new solutions. I have often been able to cobble together multiple income streams to arrive at the target income my family needs in any season in life. As I finished writing my second Ebook, I knew that I needed to figure out what my income goal was, and I knew I would figure out how to meet it.

As a private school teacher, I earned $500 a week, so that's what I set my sights on earning in 2012. It would not be enough to dig our way out of debt, but at least it would replace the income from the job that I left. As I set my earning goal, I realized that there were many different ways I could achieve the same final outcome.

Here are multiple ways to earn $500 a week:

- Earn $2000 a month
- Earn $100 each "work day" Monday through Friday
- Earn $500 a week
- Earn $67 a day for every single day of the month

In my planner, I wrote in a green Flair pen how much money I earned every day as I received it. I kept a running total for the month. I did not hit my goal in the beginning of 2012, but I was observing what strategies *did* make money and how I could achieve my income goal over time. I was far from where I wanted to be, but I was making progress. Just like my work in organizing our home, my goal of replacing and surpassing my former income would come day by day. I was taking baby steps, but I was also building the program that would change my family and my business for years to come.

Organization Project #2: The Primary Suite

In February, I got through all the spaces on the first and second floors of my home. I definitely appreciated the pared-down dining room, living room, and loft areas, but organizing my primary bathroom, primary closet, and laundry room made the biggest difference in how it felt in our home each day. When mama is happy, everybody's happy. I have always enjoyed having my own place to relax.

Mom's Condo and Passion Projects

As you will learn later, I view my kids' bedrooms as their mini apartments. Just the naming of those spaces invokes a feeling of responsibility and ownership that I love. As much as possible, I try to parent through natural consequences and logical next steps. Referring to my kids' bedrooms as apartments accomplishes that goal.

Now, if their bedrooms are called their apartments, that makes my bedroom, closet, and bathroom "my condo". We didn't have a formal rule to keep kids' items out of our adult condo space, but I found that having an "adults only" area made such a difference in my peace of mind and in my capacity to care for the rest of my family. My bedroom was mine for both the normal bedroom organization and for my passion projects.

Passion projects are hobbies and activities that you enjoy doing–to the point where time just disappears. These are things you can work on all week that light you up inside, but these rarely have a financial reward. Most adults have one to three active passion projects at one time, but we tend to hang on to some longer than others.

Over the years, my passions have ranged from a little corner library of books to read, scrapbooking stations, jigsaw puzzles, and counted cross stitch projects. I tried to organize these areas of my "condo", but didn't make much progress. Very little was decluttered, as it is nearly impossible to discard supplies from an active passion project. It's the "I'll get to it one day" factor that gets in the way when going through a passion project stash–and that's okay. Passion projects are the parts of life that give us joy and are just for fun. There is no pressure to declutter them, as long as you have space for them. Focus on decluttering the other areas of your home first and then see what space you have available to dedicate to your passion projects *after* the other areas have been cleared out.

The Primary Closet

My "condo" was hiding more hot buttons than just what I was going to do with all the stuff related to my active passion projects. It was where I kept my clothes! Go ahead and exhale. You knew I was going to get there eventually. I think closets are made of the same stuff as black holes!

The closet where you store your clothes is the one space in the house where you have 100% control over what you keep and what you don't. For me, though, that just made the situation worse.

Waddling into my closet that day, I was at my heaviest weight ever. The antidepressants that my doctor prescribed two years prior had caused me to gain 30 pounds. I do not recommend this, but I weaned myself off of the medication. Yet the weight remained. I do not regret my decision to use antidepressants. Depression is not a diagnosis to take lightly. It goes without saying that mental health issues are a very real part of life for many people. I would encourage you to talk to your personal physician if these struggles are a part of your life. Get the support and help you need to heal. You can listen to my depression story on the Organize 365 podcast episode 69.

Wardrobe Foundations

My wardrobe frustrations were about more than just the extra pounds. My mother is a true fashionista. She is dressed to the nines at all times. When she was in high school, she would sew new clothes for herself at night and wear them to school the next day!

The summer before I started high school, mom took me on a shopping spree at the mall. We went from store to store, and she taught me how to buy a whole wardrobe that could mix and match. We pushed the limits of my Catholic high school dress code, and I had an amazing wardrobe that year. Four years later, she did the same when I went off to college.

And, four years after that, my mother and I headed to the mall once more when I was engaged to Greg and we were ready to start our lives together. This time, we went shopping at more "adult" stores like Talbots and a few smaller boutique stores in my hometown of Akron, Ohio. Once again, my wardrobe was all color-coordinated and consisted of amazing and unique pieces of clothing. My mother taught me to appreciate quality, and she had carefully prepared me for dressing myself as a put-together adult woman. At the time, I didn't realize what a blessing it was to be able to purchase a whole, cohesive, coordinated wardrobe in one fell swoop.

Throughout much of my childhood, we would have been considered a middle class family. That changed when I was in eighth grade. My mother sold the business she had built from the ground up, and my father took a new job that resulted in being offered a partnership a year later. These changes led to significant financial improvements for our family. Looking back, I can see the subtle shifts that happened in our day-to-day lives, as well as the major shifts that occurred at that time. My parents now had the ability to pay cash for private high school and college tuition, when very little money had been set aside in the past. At the time, I didn't know the degree to which our finances had changed.

That shopping spree at the beginning of ninth grade would not have been possible for our family only a few years prior, but I didn't know that. I thought this was how you shopped for clothes—all at once. Having the same pattern repeated four years later before I started college and then again before my wedding, made me think this was 'normal'.

I mentioned that my mom appreciated quality clothing, right? Well, those shopping excursions weren't cheap. My mathematical mind was watching the cash register during each transaction. That high school shopping spree in 1986 was north of $1,000! The next two extravaganzas were equally impressive. My mom not only spent that much money on my clothing, but she also led me to believe that this was the way *all* shopping should be done—groceries, household projects, all of it! I don't fault my mother; she was teaching me important life skills, but the finances are not always available to support this level of investment.

If you have the means, this is a great wardrobe creation process. Invest in a color palette and style as a base, and then add on a few seasonal pieces 3 times a year to freshen up your wardrobe. Ideally, you would go through this process every four years. You will need to have a few thousand dollars to start, and an additional $200-$300 every four months to maintain this type of wardrobe. So, for most of us, this is *not* how wardrobes are created.

The shopping spree approach sounds so easy, but after we got married, shopping trips with my mom were a thing of the past. Due to our personal debt and other family priorities, I had allocated zero dollars for my wardrobe over the past seven years...and it showed. How was I supposed to declutter my closet and rebrand myself as a successful business woman at the same time? I had to start with the basics, and that meant starting at the beginning. What could I do to be well-outfitted again with as little fuss and money spent as possible?

Quality over Quantity

From my experience, when faced with similar dilemmas, most women end up doing what I did. I looked over a closet full of memories instead of functional pieces of my wardrobe. Isn't it funny what we decide to keep forever? When I was a teacher, dressing was much easier. There was always a season or a theme that would dictate my wardrobe choices. Christmas sweaters, for instance. I could easily create an entire outfit based off of a Christmas sweater when I was a teacher. I could even get away with wearing it over and over again, too!

For the record—I do not think Christmas sweaters are ugly. As a matter of fact, my grandmother and I both adored high-end seasonal sweaters. As a preschool teacher in the 1990's, I had a sweater for every holiday and multiple seasonal choices for the fall and winter. These sweaters checked off both of my only two wardrobe requirements at that phase in my life: cute and warm. Remember…I said my mother was the fashionista, but not me! My sense of fashion was under-developed, so the best thing I can say about it is that I did try to color-coordinate.

I am a terrible clothes shopper. Part of why my mother helped create and recreate my wardrobe was because I break out in a cold sweat when I go into a clothing store. I don't know how to "mix and match." I can never find an outfit in a store like TJ MAXX where you have to select one piece and hope that maybe you can find something to go with it. There *are* people who can do this, but I am definitely not one of them. Instead, I need to buy the whole outfit all at one time, preferably the one I see on the mannequin, so that I know… so I'm really sure… that it all goes together.

I have often wished that someone would create adult Garanimals. Do you remember those mix and match outfits from the 1970's? This line of kids' clothes had animal characters on the tags. Simply match the animal on your top and your bottoms and there was no doubt that you would be looking good! I have never bought Garanimals, but I love the concept. Brilliant. I have since learned that shopping at only one store or from a single brand can do the same thing! Back in 2012, shopping at *any* store was just not an option for us. Greg and I did not have the same financial situation that my mom did when she helped me purchase all those color-coordinated outfits. I had to find another way.

In order to save money, of course, I had always shopped the sales. *Only the sales.* The problem was I had been buying clothes at the last minute and on the deep discount racks for the last decade. I bought what I could find, sometimes in a panic. My closet was full of one-off pieces that didn't make any "outfits." Shopping by price rather than appearance definitely did *not* result in a cohesive wardrobe.

So there I was…Overweight. Broke. And hopelessly fashionless.

Normal closet organization advice is to purge your closet and just keep the 20% of clothing you wear all the time. Or, turn all of your hangers backwards on January 1 and discard anything you haven't worn at the end of the season or at the end of the year. That advice didn't work for me because I didn't have enough clothes to begin with…at least not enough that fit. I couldn't figure out how to purge the little I had. I needed a new idea.

Over the next few days, I slowly tackled my clothing both in my closet and in my dresser. While I was reluctant to get rid of anything, I did come to one conclusion: my 20-year-old body was gone. Even if I miraculously lost the 30 extra pounds I had gained over the last two years, there was another 30 pounds more behind that. I was a full 60 pounds over my "pre-baby" weight.

Never mind the fact that my kids are adopted.

I was about to turn 40, and my 30s had added 60 pounds to my once too skinny frame. It was time to embrace the new me. My body had gotten me through so many challenges in life that I needed to give it some grace. I was healthy, and I was here to love my family. It was time to turn my closet into a tool for pursuing my dreams, not a museum of the past.

The realization that my closet was not useful for the life I was actually living at that time came when I opened my lingerie drawer. My mother started a clothing business in 1981 called the fine line. Mom's business sold department store-quality slips and nightgowns through a network of direct-to-consumer reps across the United States.

In the late 70s, as fashions changed and became more casual, it was getting harder and harder for women to find slips to wear under their skirts and dresses. It is hard to fathom now, but back then, this was a big problem for women who wanted to continue to wear slips. Specifically, traditional women, especially those of older generations, were accustomed to having a variety of colors and slip lengths available for purchase. As department stores no longer carried these foundational undergarments, my mom saw a need in the market and began to sell them herself.

As a grade schooler, I would help my mother in the basement as she received inventory from New York. I filled big black sample cases that would be shipped to her representatives around the country. Her reps would host shows in their homes, sending their orders back to my mother. We filled orders from her inventory and shipped the items back to her customers.

The idea of wearing any slip, let alone having a variety of them to choose from, may be very foreign to you. I had been taught from a very young age that it was a natural and expected category of clothing. Not only did I know what a slip was, I knew that they came in ecru, white and black. I also knew that a "full range of slips" would include lengths that hit above the knee, at the knee and below the knee—in all three colors. I had most of those nine configurations. I kept my slips along with my pantyhose in a large, quilted Vera Bradley pouch with a button closure.

Pantyhose. Huh. I mused. When was the last time I wore pantyhose? And, why did I still need so many in my dresser?

If you are, or were, a pantyhose wearer, then you may have had a pantyhose washing and wearing system that was similar to mine. To begin with, pantyhose are expensive, so we washed them in the sink and saved them to wear again. Secondly, pantyhose will get a "runner" (because pantyhose are made of nylon or silk, they easily snag on cuticles, fingernails or furniture; when they tear, the rip "runs" up and down along the weave) at the worst possible time, so you carried clear nail polish in your purse to "stop the run" if you were away from home when that occurred. And, finally, you always had a backup pair of new pantyhose with you at all times in case your pantyhose got a hole when you were putting them on or after tugging them up after using the restroom. Oh, and obviously, we needed pantyhose in nude, black, cream, or some fashion color to coordinate with our outfit. Although sometimes tights are worn now, pantyhose were truly a different beast, definitely a relic of a time gone by.

I sat there with that Vera Bradley bag and thought about its contents. How much money was represented by the items in this pouch? The slips were from my mother's old store that she had sold 25 years ago! I didn't even know if I could replace them in 2012. And the pantyhose... why are these items so expensive?

My trip down memory lane had cost me a lot of time as I refolded the slips and tucked the pantyhose back into the bag. I started to put the bag back into my dresser, and then paused. I needed to ask myself new questions:

When was the last time I wore any of this? Before having kids for sure. Maybe even before marriage...at some of the prewedding events? That was definitely the last time I wore a slip. I knew that I had worn the pantyhose more recently, but definitely not in the last decade. Not in the last *decade*.

In what instance could I see myself needing these items again? I had been to a few weddings and funerals in the last decade, none of which required either pantyhose or slips. I went back into my closet to see if any of my older clothes warranted a slip. They did not. Huh. I couldn't wear a slip if I tried; none of my clothing was slippable!

Sidenote: At this point, I thought about my mom and her brilliant business sense to sell the fine line when the slip market was still hot. Thank goodness we've moved beyond that fashion trend!

And what if I did want to wear pantyhose? What color would I wear? I pulled out a pair to try on to help me picture when and where I would wear them and…I couldn't even put them on.

I mean…they went over my foot, but the crotch was at my knees and there was no way in the world that the second leg was going to make it and shimmy its way up over my belly.

I was feeling a little dejected to find yet another item of clothing too small for me, when I had the good sense to ask, "What size are these?!" Teenager size–that's what size! I nearly laughed aloud. No wonder they did not fit!

I emptied the entire contents of my Vera Bradley pouch into the trash without a second thought. I saved the pouch with my travel supplies and moved on to the rest of my dresser. What else had I held on to for decades because of past programming that no longer fit the life I was living today?

Once I did purge a good portion of my closet, I was left with more space and less regret. Some of what I purged in 2012 were clothes from my wonderful shopping trips with mom decades ago. It turns out that those beautiful clothes were never going to be worn again, and their presence in my closet was just a reminder of my new body size, the money I didn't have to go shopping, and the more formal life that I no longer lived.

As I got rid of things, I realized that I didn't even need a dresser! It only housed my pajamas, socks, underwear, and other memories. My old journals, notebooks, and cards were moved to a new location. The underwear, socks, and pajamas were pared down and put in my closet in bins on a shelf. I found a clothing storage system that made sense for my life and my home.

While I didn't have an amazing before and after transformation to share, I felt I was on my way to better understanding my clothing needs. I got to keep and wear the clothing that reflected all the joy in my life that came with marrying Greg, raising two wonderful kids, and running my own business. Opening up more areas in my bedroom "condo" allowed me to use that precious space for more passion projects and a small corner workspace for my new business.

I was starting to let go of my past beliefs that there were categories of clothes I "had to have," and that each room in my house had an unchangeable, predesignated purpose. I was even able to change my beliefs about what kind of furniture a "grown-up" house should include.

Getting rid of my dresser really solidified those new thoughts. I just got rid of it! And with that choice, I also got rid of the expectation that my life would continue along the perfect path that imagined years ago. I would not continue making the same clothing mistakes I had made over the last several years. I was on my way to making intentional choices in this and many other areas of my life.

The Primary Bath

Next, I tackled the bathroom. Our house has an *amazing* ensuite bathroom with a built-in linen closet and a soaker tub. A large, adults-only bathroom meant that I had a lot of storage available for all kinds of toiletries and personal care items, probably way more of those than I needed to keep on hand.

As I think back on that time, my beauty regimen was even worse than my fashion sense. It also needed to be decluttered and updated to the adult I was becoming in my mind. I feel like purchasing makeup and beauty products is extra challenging. At least with fashion, you can buy the outfits on the mannequin. With makeup, you are on your own.

I have always been blessed with clear skin. Acne was only an issue for a few months in my teenage years. And, while I love MaryKay, my makeup of choice was from Walgreens. I kept it simple and bought drugstore blush, eyeshadow, mascara, and lipstick. Always lipstick.

It is amazing how much our mothers influence our lives. As soon as I was allowed to wear makeup at the age of 16, I did. I was taught that to go out without lipstick on was the equivalent of going out of the house naked. I just can't do it.

There I was at the age of 39, and I was still using the same makeup in the same way. Twenty-three years of Covergirl: rose silk blush, champagne eyeshadow, and a plum raisin shade of lipstick. No foundation and no skin care routine. Even worse, I still washed my face with just water. I know, I know.

Since I only used a few products everyday, you would think cleaning out my bathroom would be easy. Oh, no. Just because I only used those products didn't mean I hadn't tried other products or made aspirational purchases that never were put to use. My bathroom was swimming in samples and regrettable drugstore purchases I couldn't "just throw away."

To trash it all was too extreme. To sell it on ebay was too tedious.

I decided to create 3 temporary rules.

Rule One: Obvious misses. This included items I knew I would realistically never use. I gave myself permission to throw these away without regret–as long as I didn't repeat the purchase.

Rule Two: All samples and purchases had to be tried in the next few months. I put all the options in a basket, and on the weekends, I tried new styles and products to see what I liked. The second part of this step was the true gamechanger. No. More. Samples. Period. I never use samples then, not even for travel. They always end up in the trash, but before they do, I see them and think…

Maybe this is the answer for _____.

I should just use that up!

I don't want to waste…waste what? A free marketing ploy from a beauty company? This is a marketing "gift" that is taking all of the joy out of my self-care time. It is no gift if it causes stress!

Like many moms, the time I spend in the bathroom are often the only moments when I am truly alone. I was giving that mental and physical space over to these itty bitty promotional samples that weren't even big enough to save me time or money.

Gone. Gone! No. More. Samples. Of any kind.

If possible, I stopped the samples from even coming into our house. I refused them at the store. I stopped requesting them through promotions. I trashed them directly from the mailbox before I even walked in the house. If they were added to my groceries, I pitched them as I emptied the bags when I got home.

Rule Three: To embrace and be ok with the fact that I had a very simple beauty routine. Until further notice, I would only buy those products that I knew I truly loved and used daily.

I had forgotten how powerful it was to actually give yourself some rules or boundaries. I had learned this trick with my Creative Memories clients years ago. Creative Memories is a direct sales company that helps you preserve your family's story and your personal memories in archival-quality scrapbooks. I was a Creative Memories consultant for 17 years, and during that time, I held workshops once a month in my basement.

At those workshops, women would sort their photos and create albums. As they were sorting, many would routinely ask me how many photos fit in a scrapbook. The answer was, it depends. Are you going to cut the photos down? Do you like a collage look, or do you like fewer pictures on a page? Are your photos 3x5 or 4x6 or 5x7?

Every time, I was trying to give a precise answer about exactly how many photos would fit in the album. I was worried that if I said 350 and 400 actually fit, the client would be frustrated that she didn't have another 50 photos selected. And, likewise, if I said 450, and only 400 fit in that album…it would be equally frustrating!

For a big-picture thinker, I was stuck in the details on this one. Finally, I decided to use a standard answer to everyone inquiring, that "about 400 photos fit in one album." That one decision was life-changing. Now, I had an answer ready. All my clients had the same answer and could share if I was not close by and they were helping a new client. Women started making stacks of 400 photos. I had established my rule for scrapbooking.

Decisions that I have to make over and over again are mentally exhausting. As I was asked the same question repeatedly, I started to define my decisions as "rules". A "rule" in my mind, is a decision that I have made more than once that will always have the same answer in the future. If I learn new information that makes that rule impossible or no longer true, then a new decision needs to be made. Now, I only make a new rule when I must do so.

I like being in control. I like making rules. Setting even small rules–like what makeup I will purchase–helps me feel more relaxed. I know that I can spend my mental energy on other things. Creating rules reduces decision fatigue and frees up my mind for other important things in life. I have since made rules about what I eat for breakfast, when I work on my Sunday Basket®, and what days of the week I schedule specific meetings with the staff at Organize 365.

My beauty rule in 2012 became something like this: until further notice, my makeup routine will consist of Walgreens blush, eyeshadow, mascara, and lipstick in my current color palette. This rule allowed me to not worry about trying to improve my makeup routine, to easily pass up samples and new products, and to stock up on my current colors of blush, eyeshadow, mascara and lipstick when they went on sale. Creating rules ended up saving me time and money!

It felt so good to make progress in these areas of our home! With my personal spaces and the main living areas decluttered, it was time for me to tackle the family areas.

Turning Forty

My fast-paced decluttering frenzy in February routinely filled my car with donations for Goodwill. Goodwill has always been my decluttering donation destination of choice. At first, it was because there is a location close to my home. I also liked that I could make my donations at any time of day, without pre-planning and scheduling a pickup time. While this did mean that my vehicle was the "donation mobile" for this season of my life, our minivan was up to the task.

As I continued to move my focus into the world of professional organizing, I realized that there were many people with strong opinions about Goodwill as a company. Regardless, Goodwill remains my donation destination of choice for the following reasons:

First, Goodwill not only resells donations, but they also sort and recycle items that are not able to be resold. Goodwill seeks out other programs–like textile recycling facilities–for items that cannot be resold in their stores. The idea that someone sorted and passed my discarded items on in the most environmentally-friendly way was a big relief!

In my area, Goodwill trains and employs people with disabilities. In partnership with other local charities, government programs, and schools, I believe that Goodwill has a great program for training and mentoring this population.

Some people have questioned my loyalty to Goodwill, as the company profits from those who patronize their store. After a little research, I was relieved to discover that, in my area, you can actually donate items to Goodwill through the Butler County Board of Developmental Disabilities (https://www. butlerdd.org/). The county board then provides vouchers to individuals with developmental disabilities so they can buy items they need.

There are no perfect companies, but for me, Goodwill checked the boxes I needed in order to donate to them in good faith. It allowed me to focus on making progress in decluttering my home and prevented me from becoming paralyzed by more decision fatigue. I no longer needed to put effort into finding the perfect place to donate clothing and household items. I encourage you to do your own research and choose where you want to donate your decluttered items. Once you have made a clear, well-thought-out decision, decluttering will be easier. You'll have your "Decluttering Rule" and will not have to repeatedly make decisions about how to get things out of your home.

While I was donating car-loads full of unneeded items, I also started quite a massive collection of things to put in an April garage sale. I even came up with a "Garage Sale Rule!" Anything worth more than $20 or anything that could be easily sold was set aside. I accumulated my garage sale stash in our basement spare bedroom.

In the early 2000s, I was a garage sale queen, routinely holding both spring and fall sales. I sailed through the kids' baby and toddler years reselling their large plastic toys sometimes at a profit. I told you…being an entrepreneur is in my blood! I needed to earn money anyway I could. While I knew a garage sale would not yield much profit, every little bit would help, right? So, I headed into the basement to see what I could resell.

Organization Project #3:
Storage–aka the Hot Mess Room

The first two weeks of March 2012 were spent in the easily forgotten spaces of my basement. Having a finished walk-out basement was not on my list of items my dream house would have to have, but when I saw this space, I was instantly in love. The former owners had created a mother-in-law suite in the basement. The 1,000+ square feet of finished space included a large bedroom, two closets, a full bath, a kitchenette, and a large, L-shaped living area.

My initial dream for this space was to run a home daycare center or private kindergarten when I was blessed with children of my own. I knew that having a walkout door was necessary to meet the fire code regulations. When my dream of having children and an in-home caregiving business was delayed, I started my Creative Memories business while I waited. By the time the kids were on the scene, my Creative Memories business was using the basement for monthly workshops. It was perfect for my family.

As my sales increased in Creative Memories, I was able to recruit some of my best customers to become my downlines and to start their own small businesses. Due to the fact that I was raised in a family of entrepreneurs, I easily built successful direct sales business strategies that I could share with my downline. I was combining my love of teaching and my love of entrepreneurship to help others. Unfortunately, there are often many challenges associated with direct sales businesses and they are often not very profitable. In spite of these roadblocks, I was able to develop a large team that was routinely successful in making an income. Approximately 85% of my team earned a profit using the business skills that I was teaching.

Despite my personal success with Creative Memories, the company filed for bankruptcy in 2008. I felt that loss strongly. I lost my business, and to a certain degree, I lost some of my most important friendships. Going through my own painful financial and family issues from 2005 to 2012 made the loss of my Creative Memories connections that much more difficult.

Leadership changes during the years leading up to and following the bankruptcy caused me to gradually lose faith in Creative Memories as a business. In hindsight, I can now see how the company was trying to access additional markets by changing the types of products offered. The younger, more market-focused leadership wanted to expand their reach instead of nurturing the customers who were already on board. The saying goes that "a bird in the hand is worth two in the bush." It seemed that the new leadership was more focused on the potential of the "birds in the bush" and ending up scaring away many of the birds they already had in hand.

As I entered the basement in March of 2012, I was forced to admit that I hadn't yet faced the loss of my Creative Memories business and the loss of my own identity in that community. I had been in a survival phase of life for so long. I had shut the door on the basement of our house and ignored what remained down there. The leftovers from that time in my life were physically keeping the basement from being usable, but the stuff down there was again laden with so many emotions.

There isn't a logical process to dealing with strong emotions during challenging situations. Logically, I knew I couldn't stop my parents' divorce. I couldn't stop my father from dying. The recession in 2008-2009 was also out of my control. When Creative Memories went bankrupt, though, I was angry. There wasn't anything that I could do about it! The bankruptcy of such a strong brand, with such devoted consultants and loyal customers, just didn't make sense to me. It just felt wrong. It left me heartbroken that I had poured my time and energy into this venture and yet still found myself adrift. I remember that there were many days that I dreamed about having the resources to buy and resurrect the company I loved so much.

I had to open that basement door again. I had to acknowledge that the space had only been used for my business, but that particular business was gone. My family needed the room for our next season of life. It was time for me to face that one era of my life had ended, and I needed to make the basement space available for our growing kids to make their own creative new memories.

At this point, I realized that while I had probably decluttered 30% of our total possessions, I was far from being able to declare our house "organized." I had made my list of forty spaces in our home, and I had tackled most of them. As my original plan to declutter and organize those forty household spaces was drawing to an end, I resigned myself to the fact that I was going to have to make a second pass through each one.

While the spaces were starting to look and feel better to me, I hadn't yet accomplished my original goal. As a family, we still had more stuff than we needed or used. There were still spaces in our home that didn't 'fit' our family of four. Now, with one layer of that extra stuff gone, I could start to see more clearly. We needed to get rid of even more before I could call the house organized. With this realization, I decided to only focus on two categories of items as I went through the garage and basement storage areas: donations and sellable items.

I had already set a date in early April for my garage sale, and I wanted to get as much as possible out and ready for that date. One garage sale was all I was allowing myself. I knew how much work a garage sale would be, and I knew that I would only be recouping pennies on the dollar. I needed to get my house back sooner rather than later, so this was going to be a last ditch effort to earn some much-needed money. Organization could wait; decluttering had to take precedence at this point.

Luckily, in storage areas like garages and basements, most of the job is decluttering. These are the places where things go when you're not sure what to do with them. Items live in storage areas just in case you change your mind. Storage spaces are typically out of the way, and items can rest there indefinitely while staying out of sight and out of mind.

Once you put something in storage, though, you rarely change your mind. Trust me on this. Keeping these unused items leaves you with large spaces devoted to "product purgatory." Those items are taking up space and just waiting for you to call them back into service.

Holding on to an item rather than donating it doesn't give you the time and money back from that past purchasing decision. That is usually what we want, right? A do-over. We want to be able to go back in time and change what we *did* in spending that money. We want to go back to rekindle a past passion or hobby that we invested in at the time. This hardly ever happens. Just like how we file five times more papers than we will ever need in our filing cabinets, we save much more than we actually need in our storage units, too.

My home has an ample basement and an attached two-car garage. I have a ridiculous amount of storage. As you think about your home, your storage space may be an attic, a spare room, a shed or an off-site storage unit. I am a big proponent of having a storage space. If your home doesn't have one, you might consider renting one. It's incredibly important that you think of those spaces as storage that you will regularly retrieve items from, not just a holding space for items you don't want to admit are no longer wanted or needed by you or your family.

I was in my third month of decluttering my home and was finally able to get rid of so much product from my Creative Memories business. I recycled the partial scraps and put big batches of the Creative Memories items into the garage sale pile. Just like throwing out the expired food in my kitchen, it was difficult to let go of the stuff that had been purchased with real money–money that was gone forever. I also had to face letting go of the dreams I had for my first direct sales business. I was gradually acknowledging the fact that keeping these items did not make my house better. It was time to transform this space and make room for the kids to use the basement in a new way.

My 40th Birthday

40.

The day had arrived. I dreaded turning 40. As I look back, though, I see it as a new beginning. Now, I feel so much more "me" and somehow more free than ever. But that month I felt… uncertain. I was a mom, I had lost my direct sales business, and I was still trying to get my home under control so that I could care for my family in the way I knew I wanted to.

By the time you turn 40, you've come to the realization that you are who you are, and you're the only person responsible for the life you have in front of you. At least that is how I felt at the time. Honestly, having quit my job and started on this new path ironically made me feel better about where I was headed. The last few months, I had been more in control of both my personal surroundings and my path forward. I still wasn't making much money, but our home was feeling better. Calmer. Less chaotic.

It's pretty obvious how much I loved working for Creative Memories, so it probably won't surprise you to learn that I have joined other direct sales companies over the years. Still, none have ever matched the ideal blend that I enjoyed in Creative Memories. The combination of passion, product, and purpose was a perfect fit for me. I was still looking for ways to add to our household income, and I went back to my roots in direct sales.

Although Creative Memories was my favorite direct sales opportunity, it was not my first. In fact, I joined my first direct sales company, MaryKay, when I was a 19 year-old college student. My upline sold me on how easy it would be for me to earn a Pontiac Grand Am car as a bonus! I didn't even recoup my $200 investment, but I was by no means finished in direct sales. My love of direct sales has led me to be a consultant in over 20 direct sales companies! Looking for new up-and-coming companies and starting a multilevel marketing side-hustle was like drinking water when I was in my 30's.

Early in December of 2011, I was on the Direct Selling Association (DSA) website looking for a new company to join. I had found a lot of success in the world of direct sales, and I knew I was good at both selling and building a successful team. There were many direct sales companies listed, so I needed to narrow my search. I decided that the only company that would appeal to me would be a company focused on home organization. I dug into the list, researching to find the perfect fit.

Prior to this search, I had only come across one home organization-based direct sales company. This company sold cleaning supplies and a few household organizers. Their main business model was based on an individual organizing a home for an hourly fee and sending a percentage of the service dollars back to the company. The company recommended a $50 an hour service fee with 20% going to the parent company. The company was so small that you could talk directly to the owner before signing up, so I called and did just that. "Let me get this straight. Even if I find my own client, book the service, and organize the house, I have to mail the company a check for 20% of the fee that I've earned?" I asked, incredulous.

"Yes, that's right," she said.

No, thank you.

I knew this model would not work for me. First of all, how are we going to track this? The honor system? Secondly, what about repeat business? And what if you want to charge a different rate than what is recommended? I had so many questions!

In my Creative Memories business, I had built up a strong downline of people working under my leadership. When I was ready to move on to my next direct sales adventure, I had six friends ready to come with me to this new company. With my previous direct sales companies, I would have signed on and been an instant leader in the company. But this new company didn't really have a leadership plan! The differences between this new company and the prior success I had achieved at Creative Memories was shocking to me.

After an hour-long phone call, I realized that my knowledge and experience with the direct sales business model, sales, and marketing in general exceeded that of the owner. I decided not to join. At the end of the call, she told me that I should start my own business. Within a year, the company closed.

A few months later, the owner's husband called me out of the blue. "You were going to join our company as an instant leader. You had so many ideas. Why didn't you join?" he queried.

"Your wife told me to start my own direct sales business," I told him matter-of-factly.

"That's what I thought," he said, resigned. Apparently, she had that conversation with other potential consultants, as well.

I knew I had been learning about sales, marketing and business leadership all along. That day, I learned another business lesson…

Don't be so in love with your idea that you are closed to collaborative thought.

So, there I was scrolling the DSA website in December 2011. I finally found a company in the home organization category that was still in its first five years of business! Let's call this the Organizational Direct Sales Company. This company had the consultants go to people's homes and sell them different kinds of containers and storage supplies. While I already knew that buying more cute containers would not solve an organization problem, a modest amount of products are useful in getting organized.

Once again, I saw the opportunity to join a promising, young direct sales company. And, yes, once again, I erroneously thought this company would want input from a seasoned and successful direct salesperson. I had already demonstrated that I could earn a profit and build a successful team in the direct sales environment.

I signed up as consultant #297 in December of 2011. I was ready to start selling! If you know me at all, you know that when I commit to something, I am all in!

Direct sales companies often sell through a party plan model. Think of the classic Tupperware party where you and your friends gather for good food and a glass of wine, while the business rep shows you the latest and greatest gadgets that you absolutely "must have."

People who work in direct sales tend to be extremely passionate about their products. We live, eat, and breathe the company party line. In order to sell products and make a profit, we need to get people to host and attend those in-home parties. Even back in 2012, before online sales really took over, it could be a challenge to get people together.

I had been in and supported many other consultants in dozens of direct sales companies. I knew how they worked. Despite my past experience, I was surprised at having such unexpected, amazing success with this new company. I was baffled when my Organizational Direct Sales Company parties were so well attended. I typically had 12, 15, and even 18 attendees! I wasn't *this* good. What was going on?

I went home to Akron, Ohio, to celebrate my 40th birthday with my mom and my sister. While I was home, a friend of mine from grade school offered to host an Organizational Direct Sales Company party for me.

Twenty-two people were registered for the party. I figured I would see a lot of my grade school and high school friends there. I did not. These were all brand-new customers!

"Maria, What are all these people doing here?" I questioned, both shocked and nervous. What had she told them?

Maria just smiled and said, "Lisa, everyone wants to know what a professional organizer has to say." She spun around and served another appetizer, offering to refill a friend's beverage as I stood there in shock, processing what she had just said.

I am a professional organizer. *I am a professional organizer!*

My brain went through a photo montage, just like you see in the movies. I saw scenes from my past and all of the different jobs I had completed…

- Organizing kids' play areas at my friends' houses, as our kids played underfoot.
- Making dozens of Creative Memories photo albums on commission.

Writing an ebook in 2007, *Organizing the Business of Direct Sales.*

- Transforming home offices for fellow direct salespeople, so that they could increase their profitability.

- Helping friends plan kitchen remodels so the space would work better for the entire family.

I am a Professional Organizer!

My brain felt like I had been working on a jigsaw puzzle without the edge pieces and Maria had just given me the corner pieces. Organizing kitchen pantries in my babysitting days, developing the concept of a Sunday Basket®, creating a plan to organize my own home, and helping women get photos into completed albums. I was combining my teaching background and my desire to help others get organized! I finally incorporated these two areas to reveal *my* unique purpose on this planet.

It was time to merge my past experiences and these new opportunities under the professional organization umbrella.

Discovering My Purpose

"**E**veryone wants to know what a professional organizer has to say."

During the drive home from Akron to Cincinnati, I thought through how this new realization changed my perspective. I was already getting requests to organize clients' homes at my Organizational Direct Sales Company parties, and I was charging for those services. I just hadn't put it all together to see how helping others get organized was my gift to share with the world.

For so many of us, our greatest gifts are invisible to us. The things we are created to do sometimes come so easily that we dismiss them as unimportant or common. Yet, time and again, they are actually unique abilities that we are called to share with the world, if only we can learn to value ourselves.

We are often so close to what makes us unique that we discount the value of that talent entirely. The fact that someone else assigned the Professional Organizer label to me and dozens of people validated that label by attending my in-home parties, helped me to see that my skill was a truly unique gift. It's a gift that was invisible to me until someone else gave me the label. It wasn't until then, that I started to find the value in my unique gift.

Unfortunately, I find this is true of other people, too. When I have helped someone get organized, their gift usually becomes more visible. Many of the people I have hired to work at Organize 365 are initially blind to the *amazing* gifts that they can bring to the team. I want them—and you—to see the power that comes with claiming and celebrating our individual gifts! That is the core of the mission of Organize 365.

Initially, I was deflecting my own gift by telling myself that earning a little extra money while organizing on the side or helping another direct salesperson's office streamline for profitability and productivity after a training session were all solitary, one-off events. I didn't have any special training in organizing others; I thought everyone could see spaces and stuff the way I did. Granted, there *were* a lot of one-off events during this time in my life, but putting my shingle out and declaring, "I am a Professional Organizer" took things to an entirely different level.

I mean, who am I to call myself a professional? Professional?!

I didn't doubt my skill. I knew I could organize almost any situation. What I doubted was if I could charge for my time.

Why would someone pay *me* to do this thing that came so naturally? The doubts running through my mind were thick. I had gone to college and got teaching degrees and failed at that. How could I ask people to pay me for using my self-trained skill to help them organize their home?

I thought back to my high school babysitting career. You may have babysat, but I had a career. I knew I wanted to take care of children, and I set out to make that happen. I strategically found doctors' wives and offered them my babysitting expertise. I developed a marketing plan and I was there to offer my services. By the age of 16, I was booked six days a week in the summer. My babysitting income was solid. I provided a service that was in great demand and loved my jobs.

It can be a challenge to transition from using your talents for free–to creating a profitable business and relying on that income. The reality is that we all need money to survive. Most of us recognize that certain goods and services are worth paying for, but we often struggle when we have to assign a value to our own worth.

How would I calculate the fees to charge for my services as a professional organizer? I flashed back to the conversation I had with the direct sales owner seven years earlier. She suggested that homeowners would pay $50 per hour to have their homes organized. That was a LOT of money!

It's ironic, but I had absolutely no problem charging $35 an hour to clean someone's house. I didn't like to clean at my own house—or theirs! It was gross, but I was thorough and good. I felt like I could justify charging people to complete a chore that no one likes to do, but could I be paid even more to do a job I loved?

The real truth was that my guilt was holding me back. I was also struggling with imposter syndrome, doubting my skills and feeling like a fraud. How could a professional organizer let her house get to the state of chaos that had surrounded my family? And truth be told…it was still surrounding us. Yes, the house was looking better. I was no longer tripping over things and the closet doors all closed again, but was I actually organized? I didn't *feel* organized.

What did it even mean to be organized? In my own opinion, if you were to call yourself a professional, then your home should look and feel like a glossy magazine photo shoot when you are finished. Ugh. Too much work. I was exhausted just thinking about it!!

I had been taking "before and after" photos of the spaces in my home as I went through my own organization transformation over the past few months. My intention was to post them on the blog, but honestly, the pictures didn't look that much different. The reality was that in this phase of life, my home would never be magazine-ready. I now understand that there are no perfectly organized houses—especially if people are living there.

I had left teaching and was considering embarking on an uncharted adventure, but I did not know where it would take me or how I would get there. I understood the direct sales model when someone else had already created the product, but what would it mean to do it all on my own? I wasn't sure I was ready.

Looking back, I was *way* too hard on myself. I had already forgotten the lesson about giving myself grace, and I was holding myself to an impossible standard of perfection. I was overlooking the amazing progress I had made and how much better our home was functioning for our family. We had less mess, less stress, and less chaos. I was determined to keep making progress.

Organization Project #4: The Laundry Room

The next day, I tackled my laundry room. This time, I was not only thinking about improving the function of this space, but I also wanted style.

On my original dream home wishlist was a first-floor laundry room. Despite being young newlyweds with no children to consider, this was pretty much a non-negotiable item when we were house shopping. I wanted to be a stay-at-home mom. I wanted to be able to cook, do laundry, and watch my kids–all in one space. Growing up, our laundry room was in our basement. It was a very unappealing place to go. I remember avoiding it as much as possible. During my babysitter career,

I had the opportunity to see how a family's life could flow throughout different floor plans. I knew how I wanted our home to function, and I knew that I wanted that first-floor laundry room.

The laundry room in our home is amazing! The previous owners had bumped out the entire side of the house an extra 4 feet when they were building! This added four feet to the size of the family room, primary bedroom, and laundry room! It essentially doubled the length of the laundry room on the original plan. Over the years, I have been able to add counter space and cabinets. Ideally, that area would be used for folding clothes, but in reality, it became the place where we dumped items that were waiting to go somewhere else.

I love my laundry room! This is the one space I feel like I have complete control over in every way imaginable. It is a small space and can be redecorated inexpensively, without too much time or effort. I have always loved making that space extra enjoyable for me. When my kids were toddlers, I wallpapered the laundry room in yellow during nap time one day. I was hoping to add a bright, sunny feel to those long winter days. A few years later, I changed the sunny wallpaper to a bright terracotta orange paint. None of these pops of color matched anything else in my house, but the freedom to do anything I wanted in that space helped to keep me sane during those stay-at-home years.

The constraints of the laundry room space also created a real-life jigsaw puzzle! Adding in cabinets the entire length of the wall above the washer and dryer gave me 10 feet of cabinets to organize. The contents of the cabinets changed occasionally, as the needs of our family changed. I could reconfigure the space as the items I wanted to keep closeby would change every few years.

As I decluttered and cleaned each cabinet again in 2012, I thought through what household items we needed close at hand during this phase of our lives. Over the years, these cabinets have housed cleaning products, lightbulbs, indoor tools, gift wrapping supplies, pet supplies, gifts, batteries, laundry supplies, flower vases, school supplies, and business supplies. I rearranged the items in these cabinets and tried to think like a decorator. How could I make this space more magazine photo-shoot worthy? I wanted to make the chore of doing the family's laundry even more enjoyable for myself.

Right above the washer and dryer, I decided to install a six foot-long shelf. I wanted it to be just high enough to clear the top of the washing machine and low enough to maximize the space between the washer/dryer and the cabinets above. I searched the house for a few cute, yet functional items to display on my new shelf.

I found a small basket to hold socks that were waiting for their mates. An old wicker serving basket perfectly held our plastic hangers, and I repurposed a squatty old vase to hold laundry pods. A quick tidy later and the laundry room looked amazing.

Now, I don't have to tell you how long that "perfect look" lasted. Not long. Not long at all. But, I was still learning important lessons and valuable skills about how to declutter and organize my home.

The Garage Sale

I took a quick pause from working on the house to get ready for my long-awaited garage sale. I made my way down to the basement spare bedroom to prepare the items that I had been accumulating over the past few months. As I got closer to the bedroom, I saw that the piles had overflowed into the basement living spaces. I convinced myself that it didn't really matter, because no one used the basement anyway. I walked into the bedroom, and my mouth hit the floor.

I had been tossing in anything I thought was able to be resold since January. The piles were taller than me! Literally, items had been tossed on top of huge, unwieldy piles, creating a suburban landfill inside my home. I felt disgusted. And the thought of moving, tagging and sorting all this for sale caused me to break out in a cold sweat. There was no way I was going to get through all of this stuff in five days!

"No, Lisa, stop it. You have five days; how much *can* you do? You have two choices: get it ready to sell or donate it and lose the profits. Get going!" It felt like I was awakening a New Lisa who was ready to take over!

It is so hard for me to think back now to how I used to process information during this time period. I had never even considered how my negative thoughts led me to feel so powerless. Back then, I was in reactive mode and easily felt sorry for myself. As I continued into 2012, I felt like a more mature and more positive, professional Lisa had emerged. I am so very grateful that this New Lisa is still in control of my life!

I remember the first time I heard this New Lisa. I was 29 years old. We had lived in our home for five years. I was busy cooking and cleaning, and I noticed that the oven needed to be cleaned.

Huh. How do ovens get clean inside?

I searched the recesses of my brain, and I simply didn't know. I had never seen my mother clean our oven. New Lisa said, "You clean it. Get moving."

I clean it? How?

Eventually, I remembered an ad for Easy-Off oven cleaner, so I headed to the store and bought some. I read the directions and got to work. An hour later, my oven was clean—just like that! It is silly to say now, but I felt SO accomplished. I had cleaned my own oven! Even better, I had figured out *how* to clean my own oven. I was a problem solver, and this problem was checked off my list.

I shared my big accomplishment with my friends, who ALL replied, "Don't you have a self-cleaning oven?"

"What is a self-cleaning oven?! Does a little fairy come out and scrub your oven for you?" I was serious. Self-cleaning? That made no sense.

They laughed—and then lovingly told me that a self-cleaning oven gets super hot and burns off any food inside the oven. It turns out I DID have a self-cleaning oven. And it was magical! To this very day, I still think the self-cleaning oven should be included as the 8th Wonder of the World!

In 2012, New Lisa was working her way into a permanent role. She wanted the garage sale *done* and done *on time*. Ugh.

I started by taking everything upstairs into the living room and dining room so I could see what I had. At least that worked on a psychological level because once the items were upstairs, they were halfway to being out of the house, right? I made another rule: nothing would go back down to the basement. The only problem I ran into was when I had more in my garage sale piles than would fit in both of those spaces upstairs. I *could* and *would* figure this out! New Lisa to the rescue!

By Wednesday of that week, I parked the van outside and started setting up tables in the garage. I also went to category pricing versus individually pricing each item. All books would be sold for 50 cents each. Any gift bags would be 25 cents each. Kids' toys were sorted into piles for $1, $2 and $5 each. On the day of the garage sale, I would lay out a blanket with a sign for each price point. Anything over $5 got an individual tag. All prices were negotiable. It all had to go!

I had plenty of garage sale experience, going into this final sale. While the kids were little, I spent many Saturday mornings at garage sales as a way to get "mommy alone" time. I would drive around and listen to music while searching for a great deal. Alone with my thoughts, I felt completely free. Still to this day, I feel that garage sales are financially-relevant, especially for those with kids under the age of five. Young kids generally don't often wear things out before they outgrow them, and many times kid's toys are durable enough to clean up and pass on to other families. We save money and we keep usable items out of the landfills! It's clearly a win-win situation!

Some of the garage sale items I purchased during my Saturday morning outings, were things like a Little Tikes Cozy Coupe car, Tonka trucks, baby gear, and other popular kids' toys. Many times, I was able to turn around and resell them at the same or a higher price at my own garage sale just six months later. I stuck to those big items. I didn't try to snag garage sale clothes or smaller items. I would take the profits from my garage sale and rebuy "new" garage sale toys to help entertain the kids for another six months. That same stash of garage sale money cycled around for about seven years until I just stopped in 2008. My kids had grown older and there wasn't a big demand for the items that I had to sell. Thanks to the Great Recession, it seemed like there was a garage sale around every corner.

So…the day of my last garage sale had finally arrived! This was an important day on this journey to clear out my own clutter. I could clear up space *and* make money if things went my way. My garage and my driveway were overflowing with items for sale. I knew the profit from this garage sale wouldn't cover what I had spent to purchase these items, but any income was needed at this point! By the end of the garage sale, I was very pleased with the extra $400 in my pocket. I made two trips to Goodwill with all of the leftovers. It felt so good to clean up the garage that weekend–with that job complete and those items no longer cluttering our home.

Baby Stepping into My New Career

My house was nowhere near the picture-perfect images of "organized" that I had envisioned, but our days were running more smoothly. I also felt like I had to manage fewer unexpected events that had previously derailed my day. It was time to start putting the hours and the effort into recouping my teaching salary.

Launching My Professional Organization Business

Maria's nonchalant statement, "Lisa, everyone wants to know what a professional organizer has to say," rang in my ears over and over. I had taken the month of April to start a second website, one that was just for my professional organization services. My prices were so reasonable that I quickly booked jobs and found myself constantly on the move.

Not ready to accept the fact that my services were actually worth $50 an hour, I initially priced myself at $40 an hour with a two and a half hour minimum session. I needed to earn $100 a day in order to replace my teaching salary.

Naively, I thought I could book two sessions each day–one in the morning and one in the afternoon. I quickly realized that with travel time and other family obligations, I would almost never be able to fit all of that into a day. I adjusted my approach and used any extra time I had to give in-person estimates for future jobs.

There were a host of additional problems that kept me from meeting my daily income goal. First, I was unsuccessful in booking clients five days per week. How could I possibly meet my goal if I couldn't book the clients? I really didn't want to work on the weekends, but I found myself taking clients whenever they were available. Unfortunately, this included scheduling appointments in the evening and on the weekends. I hated the fact that I was cutting into our precious family time, just to earn an income.

I also found that, though it was nice to make $100 for two and a half hours of my time, this was just not enough time to actually finish any space in someone else's home. I needed more time if I intended to leave the homeowner with a completed space instead of a half-finished area and a headache! As someone claiming to be a 'professional organizer', I wanted to leave clients with that sense of progression and completion that I was enjoying myself.

Last but not least, I underestimated how physically and mentally tiring organizing would be when done day after day. Helping other people make multiple decisions and then physically moving items around their home took a toll on both my mind and body. As I continued to grow as a professional organizer, I learned to schedule only three to four days per week physically doing organizational projects.

This new job as a professional organizer came with a lot of driving! Thankfully, I think best when I'm in my car. I turn up the music and am somehow able to turn my best ideas into a future vision. As luck would have it, I was spending 25-30 hours a week in my car driving the kids to school and doctor appointments. I was also driving myself to give estimates, complete professional organization jobs, and attend direct sales events. I literally had a part-time job—just driving! It was crazy, I know, but I tried to make good use of that time.

I've always enjoyed taking the time to process through how to best grow and develop my business and my brand. While wearing so many different hats over the past five years, I was just never able to devote the time I needed to put my thoughts into action. Now that I had more time for driving, thinking, dreaming and processing, I realized how much I had missed the freedom of feeling in control of my life and my future. I didn't have the answers yet, but I could feel the change deep in my heart. I would figure this out. I just needed more time.

Planning My Week

With all of the driving I was doing, my minivan became my second home. I never knew what my days would bring, where I would be, or what opportunities would arise during the day. I was strategically aligning the schedule of my kids' school and activities, my client appointments, meetings, and household errands with military precision. I needed to be prepared for just about anything!

On the weekends, I would use Google maps to print out the directions to each appointment I had scheduled that week. I budgeted the driving time I needed into my schedule every day. I found myself using small pockets of time at random places all over town to check off any errand that I could. Taking advantage of these 20 and 30 minute breaks required a lot of planning!

In 2021, smart phones, Google calendars, and delivery services allow us the freedom to live less structured and less planned lives than I needed to back in 2012. To be honest, I was a QWERTY keyboard lover and refused to give up my Blackberry when everyone else was firmly attached to their smartphones. Many of my friends already had the first versions of the iPhone and relentlessly tried to convince me how freeing it would be to move from my printed planner to a digital digital calendar app. I held on tight to my Blackberry for as long as I could; I wasn't quite ready to revamp my planning process!

Back in 2012, I physically wrote out my weekly plan to see where my time was going. Printing out physical directions helped me to understand where I needed to be and how long it would take to get there. Running errands in person allowed me to use coupons, spot deals, and buy items as we needed them. This was definitely helping our cash flow. This step between disorganization and productivity is the act of learning the *skill* of organizing. For many it occurs as a physical process long before it can be done digitally.

The weeks went by and I was spending more and more time in my car away from home. I would, on occasion, run into situations where I lost time or money due to lack of preparation or foresight. Each week, I got better and better at predicting what opportunities would arise during the work week when I was away from home. I did this on Sunday when I went through the actionable household tasks in my Sunday Basket®. I would take any problems from the week and find a solution so that the next week would run more smoothly. Ultimately, the solution was to pack my car for the week as if I were taking a road trip.

Today, I am a master Google calendar scheduler and have three calendars I maintain: a personal calendar, a public team-work calendar of meetings, and a private work calendar for planning how I spend my non-meeting work time. I was finally living the Brian Tracy quote that "every minute that I spend planning will save me three to four minutes in execution." The process of moving from a physical paper planner to a digital system took time. I had to learn new systems, new skills, and new habits.

My Car Closet

I was blessed with parents who could afford to buy me my first car. My father loved cars and was so excited to pick out a fun, sporty car for his daughter. I had just graduated from college when he asked what kind of car I would like to drive, and I wanted a minivan. I'm not kidding! I was *that* committed to my vision of being a wife and mother.

No one in our family had ever owned a minivan, but all the families that I babysat for had one. I wanted to be married with kids, and a minivan fit that vision. That is the car that I longed for at the age of 22, before Greg and I were even engaged. Despite my plans and gentle nudging, my father bought me an emerald green Chrysler LeBaron with a tan convertible top. It was beautiful. He knew better than I did that I didn't need to start my mom identity just yet!

I finally got my minivan when I was 30 years old, after we adopted Abby. Over the next 14 years, I was the proud owner of two different Honda Odyssey minivans. And, boy, did we drive them…nearly into the ground! Both of those minivans went all over Cincinnati, to my home town of Akron, Ohio, and on our annual drive to Orlando, Florida, where Greg's family still lived. I have hauled full-size couches and monster donation piles, and made many trips with carpool kids. In fulfilling my dream of being a mom, I was never happier than when my van was full of kids.

In 2012, the minivan was my "home away from home." I needed that car to work as hard as I did to help me juggle all the obligations on my plate. By day, I was primarily using the van for my business and household responsibilities. After the school day ended, the van needed to be available for carpool and after-school activities. Managing and organizing how I used the minivan was a fun side project for me. After my Sunday Basket® session was over and my maps for the week were printed out, I stood in my kitchen and planned out what I would need in the car during the week. After packing everything up week after week, I realized I needed to create zones in my car just like I had in my kitchen.

Thinking about my car as if it were a room in my house really helped me divide up the space in a more productive way. I used different spaces to support the different roles I was playing as I moved around town. The driver seat and surrounding areas functioned as an extension of my personal space. The driver side door pocket held my weekly maps, errand lists, coupons, and more. I quickly realized that my Sunday Basket® errand slash pockets could live in that same location during the week, returning to the Sunday Basket® to be purged and replenished for the upcoming week. It helped me so much to have all of those papers out of my purse and stored in an easily accessible location in my car throughout the week.

Today, the center console in a minivan is fixed and has a built-in storage compartment. In 2012, my minivan had a tray between the two front seats that flipped down to reveal an open storage space. Thinking through how I could use this space, I created a basket of necessities that I was often needing during my long days in the car. I included a box of tissues, a small trash can, gum, car chargers, and a few snack bars that kept me going throughout the day.

The real game changer, though, was thinking about the trunk area of my car as if it were a *closet* and not a *trunk*. A closet contains items that you need and can be changed seasonally. It also has vertical and horizontal storage. I opened my tailgate and thought about that space. I needed to find a way to utilize this area to help me organize the things I needed to get everything done each week.

I started using the headrests as a place to create the hanging portion of my car closet. I went through many different ideas and settled on using a hanging organizer that had nine 6x8 inch pockets. The pockets had elastic at the top to help keep the contents in place. I filled my organizer with tools that I often needed for organizing work, a few water bottles, sunscreen, and bug spray. Having easy access to these seasonal items allowed me to focus on what unique things I needed to add to the car each week. Each Sunday, I would load up the back of my car with items that needed to be returned, my donation drop-offs, and any other things that would be needed that week.

The last key item in my car closet was my professional organizer bag. As my professional organization jobs grew, I found it easier to have my favorite products available in my car at all times. I brought along everything I would need while I was at the home, including trash bags. As I went through the process of decluttering my own house, I found using both *black* and *white* trash bags sped up the organizing process and soon became key items that I always had on hand.

> *The car pocket organizer I used was called a gear pocket and is no longer available for purchase. If you are a member of the 100 Day Home Organization Program, you can see pictures of the car closet that I created back in 2012. Check out Lesson 90. These types of organizers are still available for purchase. Here is on available from Amazon: https://www.amazon.com/FH-Group-FH1122PINK-Multi-Pocket-Collapsible/dp/B076FTZGC5*

Trash Bags

Who knew that the color and the brand of trash bags was so important? I realized this after organizing about a dozen clients. Trash bags are super important in my line of work! Even after watching so many Glad and Hefty trash bag commercials in my lifetime, I didn't realize how much better those bags were than their generic counterparts. Years earlier, Greg and I got a Costco membership in order to save money by purchasing things in bulk. At that time, we switched from using name brand trash bags to using the white Costco brand kitchen trash bags and the black Costco brand lawn and leaf bags.

The quality of the name brand bags compared to the Costco brand bags was very similar and it was a huge cost savings, too. Being loyal Costco members, we always had a box of each kind of trash bag on hand and used that brand exclusively at our house. The white trash bag was perfect for kitchen trash, and the black trash bag was perfect for bulky donations and yard waste.

During my organization escapades at the beginning of 2012, I quickly realized that if I used the white kitchen bags for both trash and donations, I would often get confused! Halfway through a major decluttering session, and there I am trying to remember which white bag was full of trash and which was full of donations! Being the productivity nut that I am, I realized that these little pauses here and there were not only annoying, but they also caused my momentum to slow down. While decluttering in clients' homes, these pauses took even more time and momentum out of my day because my definition of trash and donations didn't always resonate with their definition.

I remember the first time that I decided to bring my own trash bags to a job. Susie and I had spent the day decluttering her closet. She was reluctant to donate anything, but after talking through it all, we had filled a few white trash bags with donations. She was confident in her choices until her daughter came into the bedroom. I was cleaning up the rest of the empty hangers, straightening up the floor and getting ready to vacuum out the closet when her daughter saw an orange shirt in the donation bag.

"Mom! Why are you getting rid of that shirt?" Kim exclaimed.

"It has a stain on it," Susie remarked.

Susie's sweet daughter opened those donation bags one by one and started pulling out the contents. Susie had to re-examine and re-decide why she chose to donate each and every item in the bag…to her daughter's satisfaction. Susie's decision-making capacity was shot, but Kim kept pulling out piece after piece of clothing. Susie ended up unpacking the bags, and we hung everything back up in her closet. I left, feeling so defeated.

I do have a personal rule. I never declutter any item when its owner is unaware the item is being donated. Many clients ask me to declutter their spouse's closets or home offices, but that is a line I will not cross. The owner of the object needs to decide when it is time for an item to be decluttered and donated. Unfortunately, though, I have seen time and time again situations where friends and relatives undermine a client's decluttering decisions, just like Susie's daughter did that day.

When I left Susie's house, I felt like she had been robbed. Yes, her closet was organized and clean, but the difficult decision making and hard work she had done was undone in just a few minutes by her daughter. Before I left, Kim was already off doing her own thing, and Susie was still looking at a closet full of clothes that should have been on their way to be donated.

Susie and I had talked through why each of those clothing items was no longer needed. Susie had a difficult time parting with anything, and her baby "organizing muscles" were no match for her strong-willed daughter's objections. Decluttering is often so much more mental than it is physical. I couldn't help but wonder…what if those donations had been in a black trash bag?

For the next few weeks, I tested my theory. If we put donations in black trash bags, could we get more donations actually out of the house to be donated? Yes. Yes, we could!

It's weird to think that such a simple change could speed up the decluttering process. Donations were literally "out of sight and out of mind" once they went into a black trash bag.

Additionally, since I brought my own Costco brand black trash bags, I was confident that the bags were large and durable enough for any project. I didn't have to cross my fingers, hoping the client would have good trash bags! These were important tools for my work, and I decided to supply myself with what I needed to be successful.

Now that I had designated black bags for donations, I found myself using the client's kitchen bags for trash. Thankfully, kitchen bags are usually white, and often come with drawstring handles to tie them shut. One day, I looped the drawstrings over the doorknob to the child's room we were organizing. I had created a large trash can, anchored in place, which allowed us to keep black donation bags separate in the center of the room. When the white trash bag filled up, I tied it shut and replaced it with another white trash bag on the door knob. It was a simple system, but it worked!

At the end of that session, we had three black donation bags and two white trash bags tied up and in the upstairs hallway. Once the room was straightened and vacuumed, I walked the white bags to the client's trash can and put the black bags in her trunk. As I left, the client got in her car and followed me out. She had her items donated before I got home. Success!

A few months later, Susie and I decluttered her closet again. We were able to get rid of the donations from our previous decluttering session, along with a few additional items that she no longer loved and needed. This time, those items were safely out of sight in a black trash bag! I found that using different trash bags in this way increased both the pace I moved through a room, as well as the level of confidence my client's had in my work. I was starting to build my own organization systems and rules.

Choosing to part with any item you own is a personal decision. I like to say I am not a minimalist or a "maximalist". I like a medium amount of stuff. We all have a barometer of how much stuff we want to have around us. You might be surprised to hear that I actually have another decluttering rule, one that seems to go against what most organizers would promote. I suggest keeping an item instead of donating it if you are unsure if it still has value. I have found personally and professionally that it is better to err on the side of keeping versus purging; however, the choice should always be left to the client's discretion.

Building Endurance and Growing my Organizational Muscles

May was my busiest month on record. I came home at the end of the day physically exhausted but mentally on fire. I was seeing progress in every area: my home was getting into shape, my business was growing, and my physical stamina was increasing day by day. Every night, I would go back to a space in my own home that I had previously decluttered, looking for more items I could donate. I found myself processing through the same questions that I ask my clients during the day:

How many lotions do you really need?
What will you ever do with all these old framed photos?
When will you read this "to be read" pile?
When was the last time you used a thermos?
How many throw blankets should you keep?
Does this even work anymore?
In the future, would you actually need this?

My desire to declutter was insatiable. I got such a high from purging unneeded items. I was shocked by the changes in my life. I slept better than ever; the physical exhaustion from decluttering and organizing was cathartic. Seeing my own home and those of my clients transformed in such a short amount of time was addicting!

Through all of the sweat, my confidence grew as my clients shared how they were feeling after our sessions. I saw the results of our hard work transform their homes and their lives. I saw families have more peaceful homes and saw their stress reduced, too. I found myself faced with the fact that I would need to raise my rates and figure out how to keep working when the kids were home for the summer.

Releasing Old Hopes & Dreams

I anticipated that the arrival of summer would reduce the number of clients who wanted to declutter and organize their homes. I would also need to reconsider my availability now that my kids would be home from school. Boy, but I was wrong! My clients wanted to use those long summer days to get themselves and their kids decluttered before the next school year. With the help of grandparents and camps, I was able to find pockets of time to keep my business going, and I used non-work days to focus on my own kids.

In the summer of 2012, my kids were 12 and almost 11 years old. I was glad I had focused on our family areas and my personal spaces during the school year. Now, I could use what I had learned to help them organize their own spaces and move smoothly into their middle school years. Summers were the times that I dedicated to teaching my kids life skills. Some years, we would also use the summer break to declutter and redecorate their bedrooms.

As a child, I loved my bedroom. It was where I spent most of my time. I would frequently rearrange my furniture and childhood knick knacks. As a mom, it was important to me to take a week out of the summer and focus on each child's room: decluttering, organizing, and sometimes redecorating. I loved decorating my kids' rooms! Every three years or so, I would paint and redecorate their rooms to match their interests at the time. It had been a few years since the last makeovers, so this was definitely going to be a redecorating year.

When my kids were young, I would listen to Dr. James Dobson from Focus on the Family share his parenting insights. He counseled the audience to divide your parenting into three segments of time. Children from birth to age six are 100% dependent on their parents for everything. The adults are typically in control. Children ages 7-12 are going through a watching and learning phase. The adults are their teachers. Teenagers move through a phase of testing out their independence. Adults become their coaches and mentors.

My experience as a babysitter and later as a teacher, helped me feel confident in parenting during the first two stages of childhood. Despite that confidence, I knew that parenting teenagers would be the most difficult. I knew that I wanted to parent in such a way that my young adult children would be able to live independently, but yet come to me for help when they needed it. To achieve that lofty goal, I felt that I needed to develop strong relationships with my kids during adolescence. As I decluttered and organized their bedrooms with them that summer, I was looking for ways to foster those future relationships as they grew and matured.

Mini-Apartments

My kids were growing up, and I needed to come up with a creative way to foster their transitions into adulthood. I came up with an approach that was similar to creating different rooms out of the spaces in my minivan. We started treating their bedrooms as mini-apartments! I wanted to give my kids the freedom to use their rooms as suited them best, but I also wanted them to take ownership of their spaces. There are many life skills for them to learn when following this mini-apartment model.

Growing up in a sparsely populated suburb, my sister and I only had a few other kids who lived on our street. We were often left to invent our own fun. I created a game I called "Big Friend." In "Big Friend," I crammed what I perceived to be the best parts of being an adult into one imaginary utopia. In the game, Emily and I were both 16 years old, because that is how old you need to be to drive. Our bicycles were our cars and our bedrooms were our apartments. I drew an elaborate map of our yard labeling the street, our driveway, and a few off-road bike paths with names similar to those of the main streets in our town. Emily and I would leave our pretend apartments in our pretend cars and drive around our pretend town. We would drive through our town and meet in the kitchen, which served as our pretend restaurant. Our game included delivering mail to the mailboxes by our bedroom doors and having sleepovers at each other's pretend apartment. The game lasted for years, and we both have vivid memories of long summer days playing "Big Friend."

Hmmm. Big Friend. I think the best part of that game was the ownership you felt for your apartment. And as a child, my bedroom and my bike were the only possessions not in my parents' control. I had been thinking about a kids' bedroom as a mini apartment since then.

The first few times I redecorated the kids' rooms, I was the one who chose the new design. What if I gave my kids that same feeling of ownership in their bedrooms and let them make decisions about the space? If I had to pick one parenting decision that most shaped the relationship I have with my kids today, it would be giving them ownership of their spaces back in 2012. We planned out the new designs, shopped for paint, and bought new comforters together. I got to work making their dreams a reality!

Joey wanted a Cincinnati Bengals theme—with bright orange walls. I said yes, but I just couldn't take 4 bright orange walls. We settled on two orange walls and two walls with a free-handed camouflage. By the time I was done, it looked so cool and was definitely a "Joey" room.

Abby chose a beautiful aqua blue that matched her eyes. The bright blue walls gave the room a warmer feel, replacing the sunny yellow from her younger days. We also took her bunk bed apart, opening up so much space in her room. She would have a single bed with an extra mattress underneath for when she would have sleepovers with friends.

I wasn't satisfied though; something was still missing. The rooms were painted, and I had decluttered the kids' toys, books and clothes. What would make this space better for the kids throughout the next few years?

New beds or furniture were out of the question. We didn't have the finances for those kinds of upgrades. That's why I love paint so much! Paint is not expensive and can really change the look of a space without breaking the bank. Both rooms had just one small bookshelf each, but they were hard to organize and maintain. When they were younger, I had used plastic bins under their beds as "toy drawers." They could easily pull out the drawers as they played on the floor. Now they were getting older and I needed a new solution.

I saw this in other houses I organized, too. Child-sized bedroom furniture was expensive and hard to repurpose. Dressers were often not big enough and easily broken over time. Desks were big and bulky and offered an awkward storage solution. Besides, my kids did their homework in the kitchen, so there really was no need for a bedroom desk.

I took inventory of what needed to be organized: backpacks, bins of toys, books, binders, make-up, video games, Legos, mementos, and stuffed animals. In the same way that I had made a lesson plan for my whole house, I made a plan to help the kids organize their mini-apartments.

In the past, I had used bookshelves as an inexpensive way to corral all of the items found in an adolescent's room. As I analyzed how the kids used the space, I determined that bookshelves had two inherent problems. The shelves were too shallow to hold backpacks and school binders. Also, the length of the bookshelf often needed to be divided, otherwise, every single shelf was a catch-all. I solved the second problem by putting fabric bins on each shelf, but the kids never even looked in the bins! Now toys were just piling up on the floor.

Ugh. Toys.

At the top of our stairs, we have a nice-sized loft. This space had been so many things in the 15 years we had lived there. It started as a nicely furnished home office for both Greg and myself. A few years later, it was transformed into the playroom. I love how it was set up. It had three matching bookshelves lining the ten-foot wall. Each shelf housed a toy category with one whole bookshelf designated for Legos. The top of the shelves were low enough to store doll houses and assembled Lego creations in reach of the kids and their friends.

This space is located right outside the kids' bedrooms. As I looked at that space in 2012, I realized that no one played there anymore–it was just a space that housed old toys. The kids and I decluttered their toys that summer, but they just weren't ready to let all of them go quite yet. Either way, they were not going to use them, and the bookshelves were not going to work in their bedrooms. I needed another solution.

IKEA Kallax Shelf Unit

The best investment I made that year was purchasing IKEA cubbies for both my kids' rooms. Affordable and available in multiple configurations, I chose to put a 4x4 black Kallax unit in Joey's room to house all of his Legos and collections. This gave him sixteen different cubbies of storage. While he still didn't play with a lot of what we saved, the sixteen cube storage system allowed us to easily sort and store his stuff in their designated places.

In 2012, it seemed like everyone was organizing their homeschool space or craft room with a wall of the Kallax shelf units. Pinterest was full of posts using 4x4 and 5x5 Kallax units to organize so many different areas in a home. While that full wall of storage worked in Joey's room, I couldn't picture it in Abby's room. Joey pulled off bins of Legos onto the floor and would spend hours building and creating. The only other place you could find him was on his bed, playing handheld video games. Abby liked variety. She has an eclectic personality and is always up, moving from activity to activity. She enjoys a variety of toys, hobbies and activities. She would need a lot of cubbies for storage, but she also needed the ability to change her room configuration. I felt like a static wall of cubbies would limit her creativity.

I decided to buy her three 1x5 Kallax units. I placed the units in a U shape on the far wall of her bedroom. Two Kallax units were used as towers on either side of the window and the third unit was placed on its side under the window to create a long, low window seat. It framed the window perfectly and gave her plenty of flexible storage space.

In both bedrooms, these new cubbies of storage grew with them as the contents changed from toys to passion projects, and from stuffed animals to school-related items. I could visibly see my kids gradually becoming young adults as we decluttered and organized their rooms a few times each year.

The kids learned how to maintain this system, dedicating one cubbie to a type of toy, item, or passion project. Their most treasured items filled the cubbies, and the rest was moved out of their rooms. This kept the potential for a cluttered mess a little more manageable. The addition of the Kallax units to the kids' mini-apartments really did add a new dimension to their bedrooms and the ability for their possessions and collections to mature with them over the years. I packed up some of the kids' toys that I wasn't quite ready to donate and headed back down to the storage room.

Hot Mess Room–Round 2

I had tackled this space once already in the spring, but ended up running out of time and energy. I figured if I was bringing toys down there to tuck away, it was time to tackle the storage room for good. I needed to make sure I had enough space for the things I wanted to store. I really wanted to create a beautiful new shelving system in my storage room, but finances wouldn't allow it at the time. I focused on decluttering the space and storing the items as best that I could right now.

Decluttering Past Careers

After spending a day or two eliminating anything that could be thrown away or donated, I was left with piles and piles of random pieces of our family's past. The only items that were truly organized were all of the pieces and parts of my past careers. One huge bookshelf housed all of my teaching materials from before the kids were even born.

I still had my original leatherette binder that contained all of the job applications I sent out during the summer after I graduated from college. I had extra copies of my four page newsletter-style resume that was printed on fancy paper with coordinating envelopes. Sitting in a binder next to that was the research that I had done on all of the school systems in the Cincinnati area; I was determined to get a job that would keep me in the same city as Greg.

I did get a job in the Cincinnati area, and Greg proposed that next February. For four years, I taught in the public school system. Each year, I had a different job and a different class-room. Despite the constant change in placement, I held tight to the hope that I would eventually be able to use the lessons that I had so painstakingly created from one year to the next. While that never happened, I still held on to *all* of my teaching materials from every single subject I had ever taught…just in case I went back to teaching and might need them again. It is so hard to let go of something that you have spent so much time and money in creating!

In addition to those old teaching materials, I also had *all* of the middle school teaching materials from before I quit my job in December 2011. Looking at that bookshelf full of my life's work, I realized that I didn't know what to do with it all. Logically, I knew I was not going to go back to teaching. But, emotionally, I could not accept the fact that my teaching days were over.

Before I had children, I taught preschool, kindergarten, and first grade. The bulk of the items in my storage room were for teaching those grade levels. I knew that these materials could be used again; however my children were way beyond the years to play with counting manipulatives and phonics games. Even today, I would love to have my own preschool, but I know it is not something that I'm going to do now or in the future.

It's one thing to actually know that I would never again be a school teacher, but it was a totally different thing to acknowledge the fact that all of my teaching supplies needed to be donated. I'm a person who likes to have options. I like all of my possibilities in front of me, so that I can pick and choose. I change my mind often. And I'm multi-passionate; I like to dig into lots of different things. Standing there in my storage room, I had to wrestle with the questions swirling in my mind. Do I want to go back to teaching? What grade would I teach? Would the materials that I had saved even work in that new job?

I knew that the reality of the situation was that I would never go back to teaching simply because that type of schedule did not work for my family. I decided that the real question I needed to ask myself, was not if I was going to go back to teaching, but could I ever use these materials in a different way? Or, is this a part of my life that is in the past? Is it time to let go?

I *knew* the answer. I was not going to use those teaching materials.

The hardest items to part with were 40 thematic preschool units that I had created. The lessons were in individual folders, full of coloring pages and preschool activities. I would say those preschool folders of materials were probably the most complete and perfect work I had ever done in my life. I had spent years collecting all of those materials and pouring my soul into creating them. These lessons were more than just physical folders…they represented a part of me.

I think I was dealing with more than just letting go of my dream of being a teacher. I was also letting go of something that I had put years of blood, sweat, and tears into creating. I wanted a return on my investment.

I had already gotten rid of the dozens of boxes of supplies that corresponded with each of those lessons but I just didn't want to throw all of this hard work and money away! It didn't make sense to donate these to a local donation center. What would they do with them besides toss them into the nearest available trash can?

How could I donate these lessons? Could I sell them? Who would buy a collection of preschool activities and what could I charge for them? Still looking for any way that we could add income to our family's bottom line, I decided to list the 40 preschool units on Craigslist and see what would happen.

Much to my surprise, I was contacted by a brand new daycare center that would be opening in the area. They were looking for a curriculum to use in their new program and what I had saved would be perfect for them. I was pricing my folders at $3 each, and they chose to purchase half of those materials. It was time for us to make our annual family drive down to Florida, and we would be passing right by the new daycare center. I told them that I could drop the preschool units off on our way. Knowing that it wasn't very likely that I would be able to sell the rest of the folders online, I asked the owner if they would like to have them all for the same price. Of course, she said yes!

Passing these folders on to bless someone else had ended up blessing my family financially, as well. The extra income would help us during our vacation in Florida visiting with Greg's family, and it was a huge relief that my hard work would not be thrown away.

I see this so often in organizing with my clients, too. It is far easier to let go of those expensive or painstakingly created items if you are certain that they will be put to good use in the future. I knew that my work would help this daycare center get their new program off to a good start. I was not only making progress and helping others, but it felt great to declutter that space with no regrets!

Decluttering Family Dreams

The next big pile of emotional memories and clutter that I encountered in my storage room that summer included files of medical paperwork related to infertility treatments, dozens of adoption books that we had read, and stacks of home study paperwork and adoption classes. And on and on.

Standing there now, having just had my 40th birthday, I realized that I never would experience the blessing of pregnancy. I remember back to when we were trying to conceive, praying that if the baby would not make it, that I would not even get pregnant. Knowing that I would likely not be able to handle that loss, God honored that request and gave us the blessing of a family through adoption.

Looking at all of those past medical bills and expenses, I wondered why I was saving it all? I had two beautiful children and a wonderful family. How was this paper and these boxes serving me now?

A few years ago, I had gotten rid of all the baby supplies we had collected. This was mostly because we didn't have enough room to store them, and the odds of us conceiving on our own were very low. Greg and I have unexplained infertility. The doctors never knew why Greg and I couldn't get pregnant. In my heart, I was always hoping one day we would be surprised with a miracle pregnancy.

Looking at that paperwork, I decided that it was time to let go of that season of our life. There was no medical information in that paperwork that would be necessary in my future. Every time I ran into these piles, it was just a reminder of a past dream that wasn't part of God's plan for us.

I was able to pass the adoption books along to a few friends who were considering adoption at the time. I saved a few pertinent pieces of information that my kids might need in the future, and I got rid of the rest.

Decluttering those piles of paper and books was emotionally draining. It didn't give me the same joy and euphoria that decluttering had in the past. I found a different kind of peace in completing this task. It was in knowing that I no longer needed to face that box or the memories it contained every time I walked into my storage room.

I was starting to see this decluttering process as more than just getting rid of things that I didn't need and moving on to the next task. I began to see that our possessions and our lives are more interconnected than I realized. I now had space in my storage room for the toys that we weren't ready to donate, as well as space to keep mementos from new memories we would make in the years ahead. I needed to keep moving forward on this journey; it was time to tackle my miscellaneous piles of paper and reach more people who were ready to reclaim their homes.

Reining in the Paper Monster

I was six months into this new journey. My Organizational Direct Sales Company parties were still going strong, but I was getting disillusioned with the home party model of selling home organization. My parties were a great way for me to find new clients, but I didn't feel that spending so much money on containers was necessary to organize and transform your home. Cute containers weren't the answer to organization. Many of the people who attended my parties wanted in-home Professional Organization services, but they couldn't afford my fees. There was a disconnect. I didn't feel that buying new products solved the problem, and the products I sold were pricey. My in-home Professional Organization services definitely did solve the problem, but the price was too high for most. How could I find the middle ground?

The true benefit of coming to one of my parties was learning the ideas I gave in my presentation. I loved teaching organizing skills, and I was looking for alternate ways to get my lessons out to the people who needed them. Sharing these ideas on the Organize 365 blog was another way for people to follow along and get advice from a professional organizer without paying professional organizer prices or investing in expensive containers. The readership in my blog was growing, but not as quickly as I had hoped. Is growth ever as fast as we want it to be?

There was something else that was missing from the blog. I am an okay writer, but it's so much easier for me to share my message verbally. My preferred way of teaching is through speaking, but the blog didn't capture the energy that I can bring to a room when I'm there with you. What's worse is that I was also getting bored. When you represent a company that has a certain product line, there are only so many things you can organize with those products. I was starting to come up with my own organizing solutions that were better than the products offered through the direct sales company that I was representing.

I determined that women were not just looking for ideas about how to get organized when they came to my Organizational Direct Sales Company parties. They were also craving the encouragement and motivation that I shared with them. The home party also provided an inspirational community of friends that could share ideas and encourage each other. I watched as they started taking baby steps to get organized, cheering one another on as they accomplished their goals.

I knew that I could successfully create a community of people learning and growing together, just as I had done during my time as a Creative Memories consultant. I started to think about how I could take the elements of my Creative Memories business… which I loved…and merge it into this new home organization idea that I also loved.

In Creative Memories, our home party was designed to expose you to storing your photos in beautiful archival albums. While I sold scrapbooking products at my parties, it was a solid commitment to this new hobby that I was truly helping my clients find. At the end of the party, if this was not a hobby that you wanted to pursue, I didn't add you to my customer list. On the other hand, if it was something that you were interested in creating and doing on a regular basis, I moved you into a monthly workshop to support you as you learned new skills and developed your new hobby.

I was finding the same thing at my Organizational Direct Sales Company parties. Some people would come to the parties and have no interest in getting organized, or they were already satisfied with how the different areas in their home were functioning. There were only a handful of people at each party who truly were ready to get organized and were interested in learning the skill of organization. As an Organizational Direct Sales Company consultant, my only available tools to foster a solid commitment to organization was to supply them with more cute containers or to encourage them to attend another party. There was no deeper workshop-type class or community available to them.

I quickly grew tired of repeating my sales presentation, so I started hosting monthly organizing workshops. These workshops were just one hour long and focused on just one part of the Organizational Direct Sales Company product line. I used these workshops to show current and potential customers how to use these products in different areas of their homes.

The first workshop focused on organizing your car. I made an agreement with a local bookstore/cafe to hold my workshop at their location. I had ten guests. After they purchased their snacks at the cafe, I gave a 30 minute presentation inside the store. Next, we all walked outside where I opened up my car, showing how these different products worked in a real life scenario.

For my next workshop, I wanted to show how to best organize a kitchen. This time, I invited attendees to my home and conducted the workshop in my own kitchen, opening all the cabinets and drawers to show how a real kitchen could be organized.

These thematic workshops allowed women to go deeper into organizing one area of their home at a time while using the Organizational Direct Sales Company's products. My idea definitely worked; I was selling quite a bit of product for the company during these workshops. The consultants in my area and ultimately around the United States followed suit and scheduled their own thematic monthly workshops. This was a better plan, but still not quite what I envisioned.

There is no doubt that I am a natural saleswoman. I was raised by a salesman who sold me on everything–from which car I should get when I graduated from college to eating my broccoli at dinner. When I look at myself as a saleswoman, though, I find that I am more interested in the *transformation* the product I am representing creates, rather than the physical product or service I'm selling. I believe that's the teacher in me. The teacher wants to see the transformation.

As one of the top recruiters for the company, I helped over 50 women join the Organizational Direct Sales Company, and I supported them in starting their Professional Organization businesses in 2012. I used the Organizational Direct Sales Company as the vehicle for getting those consultants in front of women who are interested in getting organized, and then finding which woman wanted to have in-home Professional Services. It absolutely worked! I am always brimming over with ideas because at the core, all I really want to do is help people.

The company was not very pleased with the fact that I was helping women start service-based businesses in addition to selling their product line. Ultimately, I would have loved to have been more involved in molding and shaping that company's future. By the end of 2012, I realized that I had moved beyond their business model and they were no longer interested in my 'outside-the-box' ideas.

Have you ever been at a time in your life when you found yourself struggling and you tried to go back and recreate the success that you'd had in the past? It never works the way it did the first time, does it? It's so frustrating because it feels like it should. That same experience was leaving me feeling stuck…again. I have been a member, consultant, and leader in so many direct sales companies. I love the direct sales industry, and so much of what I know today comes from the lessons that I've learned in the past 20 years of direct sales experience.

Creating workshops that were specific to the real-life use of the products offered by the Organizational Direct Sales Company was a novel idea, and not too far of a stretch. I knew that my next idea would involve stepping out on my own, without my fellow consultants. This idea was not going to be as easily profitable, but I hoped it would be extremely impactful.

The Very First Paper Organizing Workshop

Here's why I really don't encourage people to purchase a bazillion organizational containers. They are so tempting, but they are not always the complete answer to the problem. Personally, I fall in love with the cute designs, the new patterns, and the way an organized bookshelf or pantry looks with coordinating containers. I have spent the money. I have bought the products. And yes, I even have the T-shirt!

Beautiful, organized container systems don't last. They cost a lot of time and money to set up, and often need to be maintained and updated. Also, nine times out of 10, the container that I purchase for the organizational project that I'm working on is not the perfect solution. So, I change the project that I'm doing to fit the container, or I set that container aside and go purchase another matching set of containers that I think will be my perfect solution. Why are we all such suckers for the fancy, color-coordinating matching sets?!

It's just a backwards way of organizing.

It's not like I didn't know that when I went into selling for Organizational Direct Sales Company. I already had those opinions about the limits containers place on your organizing, but I also knew then that was my mission to help people get organized. Not many people can afford an in-home professional organizer. How do I make a profit working for an organizational company that is selling containers for stuff…when the real transformation needed is to just get rid of that stuff?

There had to be a way to create a community of people who are willing to pay to attend my workshops where they can actually organize their stuff. After much thought, I decided that organizing your filing cabinet paperwork was pretty close to organizing photos, and it could be done at my house in a workshop format, just like I did with Creative Memories. I just needed to find people who wanted to organize their papers in my house during the summer months.

It was actually a much easier sell than I thought. I decided to test my concept by offering paper organizing workshops from 9 a.m. to 2 p.m. on three consecutive days in July. My paper organizing workshops had a very simple set up. Each participant had one six-foot-long table. They each received pens, a pack of Post-it notes, and two paper grocery bags. We labeled the paper bags as one for recycling and one for shredding. Then, they got to work sorting. In the kitchen, I had other office supplies available, as well as lemonade and other refreshments. At the end of each session, I took any papers that were to be recycled and put them in my recycling bin and sent everyone to drop off their shredding paperwork at an office supply store that offered shredding services.

My first Paper Organizing Workshop had five participants. On the first day, three moms with grade school-age kids came to get all of their kids' school paperwork organized. I set them up as a trio in the living room. They had so much fun that they came back the next two days and kept pushing toward their personal goals. By the end of the week, all three of them had their kids' school work consolidated down to one bin each!

In the family room, a fellow direct sales leader came and organized all of her income and expense receipts for the previous tax year. She had filed for an extension and wanted to get everything organized, once and for all. She also came back the next two days and started organizing all of her other direct sales paperwork. By the end of the week, she had all of her papers organized in binders.

My final paper workshop guest was a complete surprise to me. I had advertised my paper organizing workshops on the bulletin board at my church. Much to my surprise, a nice, older gentleman signed up. He came all three days that week, and continued coming any other time that I had scheduled a paper organizing workshop over the next couple of years. He always walked in with a box of files pulled directly out of his filing cabinet, and we went through them one by one. There was definite satisfaction for me to share with others the peace I had found for myself by decluttering and organizing my household papers.

My paper organizing workshops in the summer of 2012 did exactly what I hoped they would do. They showed that people could begin to get organized in a community, outside of their home, and at a reasonable price point. The transformation was instantaneous. The laughter and the back-and-forth banter between the guests as they got their paper piles under control warmed my heart. Watching clients leave for home with empty bins, completed projects, and a spring in their step, I knew I was onto something.

Tackling My Own Paper Piles

I often say that July is the Bermuda Triangle of the year. I always go into July feeling like there are so many possibilities of what I can accomplish, yet I usually end the month wondering where all of that time went. Other than my successful paper organizing workshop week, I didn't do very much professional organizing in the month of July.

As I watched the gentleman from church go through his filing cabinet file by file at my paper organizing workshops, I realized that it had been a while since I had gone through my own filing cabinet. I made It my mission to go through every single piece of paper I had in binders, files, boxes, and anywhere else in my home. Not wanting to miss the warm summer days at the pool, I took my paper with me. Yes, that's right. I was the mom. At the pool. With the box full of papers. I've never been one to worry about what people think or say about me. I mean, I want people to say nice things about me, and it hurts me if they say mean things, but I also want to do what I want to do when I want to do it. That summer, I wanted to organize my paper and go to the pool at the same time.

So I did. I boxed up 10 to 15 files at a time, put the kids and the pool bags in the car and drove to the pool. While my kids were swimming and I was enjoying a fountain Coke and ice cream drumstick, I went through my papers, file by file, purging everything that was no longer needed.

At the end of the day, the kids were tired from swimming, I had a nice, golden tan, and another 15 files were purged. When I arrived home, I would toss one pile in the recycle bin and add anything that needed to be shredded into my shredding pile.

Paper sorting is so tedious. The number of decisions that you have to make in sorting through just one file folder is about ten times the number of decisions that you need to make when you organize your clothes. Chunking away at the mountain of paperwork I had saved over the last fifteen years was done in all the nooks and crannies of time I could find. I sorted paper while watching TV at night with Greg or while we were on the back deck in the evenings after work. Basically, if I wasn't working or doing housework, there was a paper in my hand that was being sorted.

Honestly, I was surprised with how long it took. Looking back, I had greatly underestimated how much paper was hiding in my home. Granted, I did have my father's estate paperwork from a few years prior, in addition to all of our tax returns and supporting documentation all the way back to Greg's very first tax return filing in 1985. Add to that a filing cabinet that was overflowing and had never been touched…well, there was a LOT of paper. It took the whole month of July, but by the time August 1st rolled around, our paper had been purged!

This experience showed me what I needed to be able to share with my paper organizing workshop clients, too. Paper is a beast. It takes a long time to tame! You need to tackle it over a long time. Don't get impatient with yourself when you attempt to make progress in this area. It always looks much worse before it gets better. I tamed the Paper Beast in my home, and now my paper is both organized and portable. Every minute I spent on this project was so worth it in the long run.

While I had proven that a paper organizing workshop would provide the transformation in organization I was hoping to find, and I had gone through all of my own personal paper in the month of July, I still didn't think I had the right paper organizing solution just yet. Something was still bothering me about my filing cabinets. I knew it would take more time to tweak this system. In fact, it would take me another five years to come up with the true solution that I share in my 2020 book, *The Paper Solution*. I chose to move my focus back into home organization and double down on that as we headed into the fall of 2012.

Start Here: The Four Spaces to Get Organized First

I love to plan out my fall while still in the summer months. For the last few years, all of my summer planning energy had gone towards planning my own school year as a teacher. During the summer of 2012, I was finally able to think about what I was going to do in the fall when both of my kids went back to school and I did not. With much of my year of personal organizing completed, my goal was to continue to grow my new Organize 365 business.

I was finally to the point in my home where I no longer opened cabinets or drawers and saw spaces that needed to be decluttered and organized. In fact, most spaces in my home felt "finished". I wouldn't say that my house was 100% organized, but I felt like I was really on top of my game. For the first time in probably seven years, I felt like I could proactively plan my fall and that my plans would actually stick this time! It's amazing how easier it is to deal with emergencies and urgent situations once you get organized.

I knew that I was not going to continue with paper organizing workshops into the fall, and I had tapered off doing thematic Organizational Direct Sales Company workshops. I knew that my time with Organizational Direct Sales Company was coming to an end; what was I going to do? I still needed to bring in income for our family.

The fastest and easiest way to make money is to provide a service for someone else. Based on past experiences, I know that most successful businesses started in some way, shape, or form by providing a service to someone else. Before all of my in-home organizing jobs dried up in the month of July, I was getting close to replacing my teaching salary. I knew that if I were just more clear about what services I was offering, then I would be able to replace or exceed that salary in the fall. I needed to focus on my unique gifts and build my business around them.

Starting my Professional Organization business earlier in the year, I had accepted any and every organization job that came my way. I loved the variety that this provided, as well as the daily challenge of tackling new spaces. I discovered that marketing my organizational services online was harder than I thought. No one googles "find a professional organizer." People want to have a specific space organized, not to hire a professional organizer. I needed to refocus my organizing efforts.

I love organizing all the spaces inside a home and even those inside a business office space, but that didn't sound like the narrower niche I'd need to make my service more marketable. I needed to define my scope and become known for something specific. This brought me back to the idea of transformation.

What spaces, when organized in the home, provide the most transformation for the head of household?

What space, when organized in my home, provided me with the most sense of calm and well-being?

Honestly, to get your whole house organized with a professional organizer would cost thousands of dollars. And while I was totally up for that challenge and able to deliver on it a few times that fall, most heads of household had a limited amount of money they could use to get a project done. I needed a way to help my clients see a greater transformation and know the value that my professional home organization service could offer their family. I needed them to understand that this is an investment of time and money. I needed to consider how to create packages of organizational services and relook at how I had been setting my fees.

Previously in the spring, I had had two different clients who had me scheduled once or twice a month. During that time, we organized many different spaces in their homes. Through working with them, I found that two and a half hours was not enough time to get a project completed. I could get a space organized in two sessions with even a little bit of extra time left over to work on another space in their house. Four hours was the amount of time that it took me to organize most spaces in someone else's home. Organizing a kitchen was another story—I needed to allow eight hours in order to complete this entire space because it is always the center of the activity in a home. At this point, I decided to increase my hourly fee and require a four hour minimum session. I had seen the difference this work was making in my own home, and in the lives of my clients. I knew my services were worth every penny!

My confidence was growing, and I was confident that I could complete projects during these longer sessions. Now, I needed to choose which areas of the house, when organized, would provide the most transformation for the head of household? Was there a particular order that these rooms should be organized? Where should I start?

I determined that the four spaces that were most important for the peace and well-being of the head of household were the following:

- Kitchen
- Adult closet
- Laundry room
- Home office

I would start in the kitchen. Everyone notices when you organize your kitchen. Many people feel like their spouse and children will not maintain a system that is set up in the kitchen, but I find that they almost always do! The kitchen is often the center of the home; we spend 80% of the time that we're home in the kitchen. We start our day making morning coffee, followed by breakfast, lunch and dinner. In addition to eating, we wash dishes and congregate to talk about our day. Most holidays are spent in or near the kitchen, as well. It really is the heart of the home.

By picking the kitchen as a starting point, I also guaranteed that the freshly organized and transformed space would be immediately noticed by friends, spouses, and children. This was an important step in helping clients develop that solid commitment, stay motivated, and continue transforming their homes. My first organizing clients were almost all exclusively stay-at-home moms. Their spouses were supportive of their decisions for how to run the household and what needed to happen, but it always helped if they could *both* see the results after the first day.

That fall, a handful of women got all four of these spaces of their homes organized with me in four organizing days. Most scheduled these sessions for one per month. By the time we got to Christmas, they were feeling so much more organized!

Is Home Organization "Women's Work"?

If there is one thing that I receive negative comments about, it is the fact that I focus on helping the female head of household get organized.

It's true, I have continued to focus on women at home and not the growing role men are playing as the male head of household. The answer is fairly simple. While I agree with, and applaud, men for stepping up and sharing in the day to day running of the household and the partnership required to turn a house into a home, women tend to view their role at home differently.

Home organization appeals to all generations. Each generation has inherent biases in how they view housework and who should take on that responsibility. So many things influence our expectations in these areas: TV shows, social media, your parents and family members, what state you live in, your country of origin, and your ethnicity.

As we continue to acknowledge diversity within our culture, our view of housework and where that responsibility lies will continue to evolve and change. The reality is that the change we see in the world will come more slowly in our homes. The way we divide housework requires discussion and a change in how we think about the roles we play at home. Addressing a change in mindset must come first; our lives are more habitual than we might care to admit.

I have said for years that men are not holding women back… our homes are holding us back. Women hold ourselves to an almost unattainable standard in our housework. We do chores no one notices, simply because we feel that those efforts make us a good homeowner, wife and mother. The idea that housework is "women's work" is an idea that was caught, not taught. You are more than halfway through this book, and you have learned very little actionable organizing. Your house will not be organized when you are done reading. This book is about my mental change that occured when I decided to take control of my home. The physical work is important, but it is the mental change–the change in mindset–that has lasting effects.

The physical act of organizing a house can be completed by a professional organization company in a matter of days. I completely agree that anyone–man or woman–can complete that task. Housework is not gender-specific, but in our American households, the role of housework defaults over-whelmingly to women. When their homes are not neat and tidy, women feel like they have failed. Men do not have that same feeling of ownership, expectation, or judgement from society. Again, this is generational, and it is changing, but it is a very slow change.

Men and women have different ideas of what constitutes "good enough." They also have different ideas about what makes a perfect home. For example, you have probably heard the statistic: Men apply for a job when they meet only 60% of the qualifications, but women apply only if they meet 100% of them. The finding comes from a Hewlett Packard internal report, and has been quoted in *Lean In*, *The Confidence Code* and dozens of articles.

Stay with me. In my family, I am a fourth generation female college graduate. My mother, grandmother, and great grandmother all were entrepreneurs, each owning a profitable business. My father did not have a college degree. Through hard work and persistence—and the benefit of a great personality, he eventually became a partner in a company where he worked. Every family member before me, male or female, had earned incomes and worked outside of their homes.

At the same time, in every one of these households, 100% of the housework and childrearing was done by the female head of household. Today, my husband and I both work outside of our home, yet we share the majority of the housework. It took us both a lot of work to get to that point. We examined how all of the household-related tasks previously ended up on my plate and what we needed to do to change that.

It started in 2012 with me giving up my career to come home and get our household back in order. Over the next five years, I reduced the work that was necessary to run our household, and we slowly began to share the household tasks. It was not smooth or easy, but we both worked together to make it work for our family.

Today, Greg does almost all of the grocery shopping, cooking, meal planning and Sunday dinners. He handles the majority of the household work and maintenance that happens in the yard. He handles drycleaning, trash, and anything car-related for our family. He is our dog's primary parent. This is the result of making the housework explicit, as well as the result of much negotiation to find a way to share the load of caring for our family. These are keys to our success, and they will be necessary for your household, too.

Think about making housework "explicit" as I mentioned. What does that mean? Well, how many tasks are associated with cooking dinner? Even when another household member helps out by "cooking dinner" one night, what actually takes place? Cooking dinner every night requires meal planning, grocery shopping, preparing ingredients, the actual cooking and assembly of the dinner, and then serving and cleaning up the kitchen. It also includes putting away clean dishes from the dishwasher or drying rack. There are SO many steps to creating even a simple dinner at home. When someone steps up to help by physically cooking dinner, that's great, but it is only a fraction of the work or effort that is involved. And yet, when another household member pitches in with cooking dinner, that's usually all that person does, leaving the female head of household completing all the other steps, while the itinerant cook gets the praise for the meal.

Think about other household jobs that have similar steps. When you make housework explicit, by recognizing all that is actually involved and adding all the unwritten steps to the division of labor in the home, it is far more likely that this kind of change will be successful.

Women are struggling. They are struggling with the unrealistic expectations they have placed on themselves as the female head of the home. They struggle with how to have a conversation about sharing the workload with their spouses. Frankly, they are too busy trying to do it all to stop and think about how to change it or even what to change. It's exhausting to simply write down all those unwritten steps for every action item to be able to tell someone else what to do.

Eve Rodsky's book *Fair Play* is a great book to identify all your household-related tasks and start the conversation about achieving a more equitable balance at home. You might be surprised as you consider the mental load, as well as the physical actions that are involved in running a household. You feel these responsibilities. You know they are there, but it is surprising when you actually articulate them and start those important conversations with members of your household. Rodsky talks about how "owning" a task includes conception, planning, and execution. The mental load that many women carry can be more fairly distributed if both partners understand and take responsibility for *all* of the steps of a task, not just a single step out of the whole process.

Do you know why teachers absolutely hate to be out of their classrooms, even for half a day? It takes longer to make the plans for a substitute teacher than it does to just stay there and schedule any necessary appointments for the summer months. Writing out all the steps and commenting on all the different aspects of the schedule, the students, and the curriculum—in other words, being explicit with all that goes into a teacher's day is exhausting. I don't know of any teacher who plans for a fun personal day off of work, simply because it is just not fun to spend the extra hours making sure that everything will be accomplished while he or she is gone.

This is the same reason why many women never approach dividing housework with their spouses or other family members. It is just too much work to explain or help prepare for someone else to do. It ends up being easier to just do it yourself. When that happens every day, over time, there will always be a physical and mental struggle that happens when the load becomes too great to bear.

It has been my experience that women internalize their perceptions of themselves based on how their homes look and function. Men see a mess and either deal with it or step over it. (Or, let's face it, guys! Sometimes you don't even *see* the mess!) Women see a mess and beat themselves up inside that the mess even exists or that someone else actually created that mess and didn't bother to clean it up themselves! It is just not an apples to apples comparison.

Should housework be shared more equally? Yes.

Is it? Not yet.

How do we get there? In my opinion, we need to give women the grace, the support, and the tools they need to objectively view all of the housework on their plates. We need to support them as they reduce the amount and streamline the workload, moving forward in a partnership. To get there, women need to know what they want, why they want it, and they need to have the tools necessary to learn the skill of organizing.

Stacking Golden Windows

The beginning of the school year has always felt more like the beginning of a new year for me. Back to school shopping, getting new school supplies, and getting my closet ready for fall always puts a pep in my step. I love the fresh start that a new school year has to offer.

As a child, preparing for a new school year was always a much bigger deal to me than celebrating the glittery Times Square ball falling at the end of December. As a teacher, I loved starting a new school year in the fall after spending the summer marinating in my new ideas for the classroom; I was ready to go on Day One.

This year, I wasn't going back into the classroom; I wasn't going back to school at all. Nevertheless, I found myself deep into planning for the fall as I flipped my calendar over to the month of August. My schedule might be different this year, but my kids were still starting school at the end of the month. That prospect had me feeling like the possibilities were endless for this "New Year" that I was starting.

And, I knew I wasn't the only one who was feeling like September was going to give me a new lease on life. A friend of mine was contemplating what to do with this school year as her youngest child was starting all day school. It was the first time in 13 years that she would not have a child at home during the day.

"Don't go back to work just yet," I suggested. "If your finances will allow it, spend this school year focused on your house. Make the transition from being a stay-at-home mom to a part-time working mom next year, after you reset your house for this next phase of life."

Her husband agreed with this plan, and we both spent that school year going through our houses, room by room, preparing ourselves for whatever came next. I was so grateful to have a "lesson plan" for this friend to follow, as I grew into my role of professional organizer and teacher of organizing skills. It is always easier to teach something the second time around. You learn from your previous experience and are able to better anticipate trouble spots. As a teacher, I had been paying attention and taking notes as I walked through that process in my own home, and then in the homes of my clients.

There are times in our lives where we have the opportunity to take advantage of unique circumstances and make that quantum leap into the next phase of our lives. These seasons are what I call "golden windows" of opportunity. There are many golden windows that present themselves over the course of our lives. Some happen every year, while some happen only once in your lifetime.

Three times each calendar year we have a "new year" feeling, providing additional golden window opportunities to restart your year. I think about these golden windows that appear each calendar year as "annual" golden windows. They arrive for all of us regardless of family size, type of work, or age.

The first and most obvious annual golden window is the changing of the calendar from one year to the next. As we celebrate the end of one year and usher in the new year, we set new goals for ourselves personally. We also set the resolutions that we want to achieve in the coming months.

The second annual golden window comes at the end of May or the beginning of June, as we transition from spring into summer. In the United States, this summer window usually includes the time between Memorial Day and Labor Day (roughly May through September). I have determined that it doesn't matter whether you work a nine-to-five job or you're a stay-at-home-mom. We still all view summer in a little different light. The longer days and shorter nights give us more energy to tackle different kinds of projects during the summer months.

The final annual golden window is the one I was experiencing in August. It's the anticipation of the cooler days of fall, teaming up with the productivity that comes when the kids head back to school. The natural hustle and bustle of life that propels us all forward starts in August and gets into full swing by the time we flip the calendar to September. No matter your age, the beginning of the school year always feels like a fresh start.

Outside of the calendar, I have noticed that several events in my own life are golden windows that give me tons of organizational energy. As my Professional Organization client roster grew, I noticed other similarities in the women who were calling me to work with them. Significant life events would often present as golden windows for organizing their homes before they moved to the next phase of life. Those could include moving, having a baby, getting married, getting divorced, having your youngest child start school, sending a kid off to college, or taking a new job.

I was preparing for a new phase of life, too—that of a self-employed business woman. I had been on this new journey for the last eight months, but for some reason August felt like a new beginning for me. I had the next nine months to develop and grow my business while the kids were at school. I didn't want to waste a single minute of that time.

I spent much of the month of August focused on my children, getting them ready for school, and enjoying the final days of summer with them. It was such a weird feeling to not be setting up my own classroom and going back to teaching myself. Organizing and setting up the classroom for the beginning of the year was one of my favorite things to do as a teacher.

I also had some apprehension about giving my business 110% of my attention come September 1st. There could be no more excuses; it was time to sink or swim. For the first time in a long while, I felt like I was gaining forward momentum and traction in my life. My house was nowhere near perfect, but my days were running more smoothly, and I was enjoying the amazing feeling of accomplishing my goals.

Creating "Adulting" Launch Pads

I am a project-oriented person. I do not like sitting idly by or waiting for people. Truth be told, most of my "playing with the children" time in the toy room when they were young was actually me decluttering and organizing toys while the children played around me. I'm either in motion or asleep.

The month of August was spent supporting my kids as they got ready for the new school year. I was committed to being proactive in setting Joey and Abby up for success and in ensuring I would have time and energy for my business. We decluttered and organized their rooms (again!) Isn't it funny how we always think their rooms are going to magically stay organized? We went back to school shopping again. We bought new clothes and new shoes and new prescription glasses again. It's also funny how we are always surprised how quickly children grow. Especially preteens! Just like most middle schoolers, my kids wanted to handle their own back to school purchases, but I stayed close by to answer questions and provide the support—and money—that they needed.

The majority of the support that the kids needed from me was in and around their bedrooms. My bedroom and closet were already organized and working fairly well. It felt really good to have worked through so many of the spaces in our home. I was not ever going to reach perfection, but I could definitely see my continued progress.

I needed to find an upstairs project to focus on so I could be nearby while the kids prepared for the next school year. Standing in the hallway between their bedrooms, my only organizational project options were to tackle their shared bathroom or the small linen closet in the hallway.

My kids' bathroom is the bane of my existence. I'm neither a germaphobe nor a clean freak, but middle school kids are just not very tidy. It didn't help that the kids were 18 months apart in age or that we had a boy *and* a girl. This was a recipe for disaster and daily squabbles. So much had to happen…in such a little space.

I thought to myself, "What do the kids really have to *do* in the bathroom? What is optional or could take place in another location? How can I make this space functional for both kids for the next six years?"

The important thing to note is that I always stop and analyze how we *use* our home. We are not limited by the traditional home areas or how a builder has designed our physical layout. I think that became much more clear during the covid-19 pandemic, as we all made adjustments to how we live inside our homes. I have always believed that it is crucial to ask questions about how to use a particular space. Part of this analysis is always to think about your current family and physical set up, and to envision how it might need to change as your family changes.

I start by imagining my ideal solution. Visions of moving to a new home where each child had their own bathroom filled my head. I had been seeing those same visions for the last decade, but there was no way that was going to happen. This was still my dream home, and I knew how much time, effort, and money it would require to move. Instead, I let my mind wander to all of the other possibilities like adding on to our house or modifying the bathroom we already had.

When my daydream was over, I faced reality. I had zero budgeted for this project. Dealing with the existing bathroom, how could I solve this problem?

Was this the only bathroom available to the kids? No. They can go to the bathroom in some of the other facilities we have in this house.

What do they need to use this bathroom for?

The obvious answer is that they go to the bathroom in the bathroom, but we have other bathrooms that could be available for that. Showering. The kids had started to get in the habit of asking if they could shower in our bathroom. I always said no. Occasionally my husband had said yes.

This was a slippery slope I did not want to go down. Our bathroom does not have a door; the space opens directly into our bedroom. This means that when the kids are in our bathroom, I can't even be in my bedroom. This was not a workable solution for me. I also knew that if I didn't nip this one in the bud soon, I would be sharing my bathroom with my kids for the rest of my life. No, thank you!

Growing up, our entire family shared one bathroom. We did not have the luxury of having an adult bathroom and a kids' bathroom. An extra bathroom was one of the first things my parents added to my childhood home when they made home improvements. Having an adult bathroom separate from the kids' bathroom was a big selling point for me when Greg and I purchased this house before we had children.

Okay, so the kids' bathroom was needed for going to the bathroom and showering. Anything else? Brushing teeth. Yes, both kids brushed their teeth at night in the kids' bathroom.

We had options, though. I was open to having them brush their teeth in the morning in the bathroom near the kitchen. This would allow one child to brush teeth and one child to shower at the same time *without* being in my bathroom!

There! I had it. I had all the pieces to the puzzle of the kids' bathroom. These were the three essential bathroom activities and of those three activities, taking a shower was the only one that *had* to be accomplished in this one location. Going to the bathroom and brushing teeth could be done in the bathroom downstairs. Great! What else were the kids doing in this bathroom that could be completed elsewhere? That list was much much longer. Grooming and makeup. Where else could those things happen? I really didn't want to move these activities to the first floor bathroom. That would mean that I had to clean up that bathroom every day in case I had people visiting during the day.

While my rule up to this time had always been that all makeup was done in the bathroom in order to save our carpeting, was I willing to change that rule now in order to keep showering the priority in the kids' bathroom?

Yes. Yes, I was.

The next part of the puzzle was to figure out how to have Abby *want* to do makeup in her bedroom, instead of in the bathroom. The biggest advantage of doing your makeup in the bathroom was the large mirror and the bathroom lighting. I figured that if I bought her a makeup mirror and put a large mirror on the wall in her bedroom, she would be agreeable to doing her makeup in her bedroom. She already stored most of her makeup in her bedroom anyway.

The time that I took standing in the hallway that day saved my sanity the next school year and beyond. Of course, I still had to clearly state and enforce the rules, but knowing what I wanted and why I wanted it helped me come up with a solution. Relocating some of their bathroom activities took the stress and emotion out of our highly charged school mornings.

I moved on to face another teenage frustration: the kids' linen closet.

I didn't think about it when we bought the house, but after organizing so many homes, I realized how lucky we were to have an adult linen closet in our bathroom and a kids' linen closet in the hallway between their bedrooms.

Well, maybe I wasn't so lucky. Having that extra area to store items for the kids' rooms allowed me to keep much more than I should have in that space. As a child, I loved having flannel sheets on my bed. I changed them to match the season; I had Christmas sheets, winter snowmen and even teddy bear sheets for the fall. I thought my obsession with warmth had trickled down to my kids. I wanted to share my childhood delights with them–what parent doesn't? Nevermind the fact that Abby didn't even like flannel sheets.

When I actually looked at what was in that linen closet, I was staring at eight pairs of flannel sheets for two twin beds. I had purchased flannel sheets for them in their favorite colors and themes. My sister had passed on her childhood flannel sheets "for the kids." I thought about how we acquired such a stockpile and got very ruthless in deciding what to keep.

Time for a personal confession. Um, we don't change our sheets very often. When we do, I often strip the beds and wash the sheets, putting the sheets back on the bed all in the same day–instead of folding them for storage in a closet. As a matter of fact, when was the last time I used any of the sheets from the linen closet on a bed? I couldn't even remember.

I stood there, looking at the piles of sheets, wondering why do we have so many sheets? We had eight sets of *flannel* sheets alone. How many do we really need? When would I ever use any of these sheets? I finally determined that we would only need a fraction of these sheets, even if our whole family got sick with a stomach flu at the same time! It was time to donate the sheets.

Side note–homeless shelters are always looking for twin sheets and old towels. Animal shelters will typically take them, too– even the ripped and stained ones.

I had spent eight months going through this house space by space, but I kept finding spots here and there that still needed attention. When you start your own organizational journey, you will find these spots, too. This was the latest surprise. Some days, you just finally see things from a different perspective, and you make a new decision. Throughout this year, I kept returning to the areas in my house that I had already organized and refined them further.

When you are decluttering, I recommend going through the same areas of your home multiple times. Sometimes you need time to be able to see your spaces and your stuff differently. Returning through areas like the kitchen in different seasons of the year helps you see more clearly what you actually use for various holidays and times of the year. You can't organize when you have too much stuff, not even if it is snuggly flannel sheets that remind you of childhood.

Parting with my childhood flannel bed sheets was harder than I thought. Not only was I no longer a child, but my own children had also passed some of the phases of childhood I held so dearly. They were growing up.

And stealing my stuff!

Ok, maybe not "stealing" but permanently borrowing, often without asking!

While the kids weren't using eight sets of sheets, they *were* helping themselves to all kinds of toiletries and grooming tools.

Hairbrushes, hairspray, makeup remover, nail polish remover, nail clippers and even deodorant–ew!

Oh, I was hopping mad! Of course, I never knew about the "borrowing" until I went to dry my hair… and my hairdryer and brush were missing from my bathroom. Or when I went to take off my makeup…and there was no makeup remover.

The first few times this happened, I may have thrown an adult temper tantrum.

"Why do the kids have to take *my* stuff?! Why can't they use *their* stuff?!"

Staring at the kids' linen closet that was half empty, both the problem and its solution hit me right between the eyes.

The problem was not toiletries. The problem was that the kids were not able to anticipate when they would need more of their basic grooming necessities. By the time they realized they needed more deodorant or more hairspray, they lacked the cash and car to go get them.

Not only that, but their bodies were still changing so quickly that they weren't able to anticipate their needs. They weren't intentionally stealing *my* stuff; they just didn't always have some of their *own*.

Ugh. I felt terrible. Can you imagine your mom losing her mind because you needed to trim your toenails? Yeah, not cool.

Having survived adolescence myself, I had an idea of what was coming and what the kids would need in the near future. It was time to stock their bathroom with supplies for teen-agers. They needed their own hairdryer, brushes, soaps, and deodorant. Lots of deodorant!

Later that week, we went to Walgreens. I chose Walgreens because it's a smaller store located close to our home. I wanted to focus on just bathroom items, and Walgreens would have them all without the overwhelming amount of other things that we would encounter at my beloved Meijer. Our single mission that day was to find a deodorant that each child would actually use on a regular basis.

I started opening deodorant sticks, sniffing, and then pushing the sticks under each kid's nose.

"Do you like this one? How about this one?"

At first they just backed up and gave me that "mom has gone crazy" look.

"This one is nice," I sniffed and then thrust my hand forward. "It smells like a teenage boy."

Joey laughed and took a long sniff. He rolled his eyes.

"Look, you can pick or I can pick, but we are leaving here with deodorant. Abby?" I pushed a "powder fresh" scent her way.

"Ew," she said. "That smells like an old lady."

Hmmm. That was my scent! I was ready to say something when I noticed the kids were finally getting into it. Sniffing and thrusting deodorant sticks at each other.

And then we all started to giggle. I stood back to take it all in. The kids were growing up. It was time for my parenting style to grow up, as well. These kids needed support and guidance as they started into their teen years.

We left with a ridiculous number of deodorant sticks. We had a variety of scents for them to try until they found the deodorant that was best for them. I still wonder what that cashier thought with us buying so much of one product and giggling the entire time. In hindsight, it probably wasn't ok for us to open and sniff those deodorant sticks in the store. I don't know how else you would do it with two moody teens. You'll be happy to know that the rest of our toiletries we have purchased without sniffing.

By the end of the month, the bathroom was stocked with the toiletries the kids needed. I also took a solo trip up and down every aisle in the Walmart bath and beauty area, ready to fill their linen closet with extra toiletry needs. Doesn't it feel so great to go shopping with a purpose? I knew what I needed, and I was on a mission. I also knew what products the kids needed, I knew where it would be stored, and I knew that they had the space for it. All of this was in anticipation of, rather than in reaction to what was coming for my precious teens. That's the kind of feeling I could get used to; I love being proactive. *That* is the feeling of being organized.

The kids' linen closet that used to house so many unused items, was now our in-house teenage store. When supplies were needed, Abby and Joey knew to check the linen closet first before they went into my bathroom. As the summer drew to a close, the kids were ready for school, and I was ready for my first fall running my own business.

Organization is a Learnable Skill

"**L**isa, you have to come back! All the spaces you helped me organize in the spring are UNorganized!"

Uh oh. My arms felt heavy, and I had a sick feeling in my stomach.

All the areas that were organized in the spring were already a mess? What was I going to do?! I had taken pride in the fact that my individualized style of organization was unique in that the spaces we organized stayed organized.

I know I had only been officially organizing for less than a year, but once I took the time to really think about it, I was able to identify organization jobs I had completed as far back as a decade ago. I took pride in being able to analyze *how* people were using their homes and helping them find organizational solutions that were tailored to their needs.

Teaching the Skill of Organizing

The first client space I remember completing was at my friend's house. Her daughter was around 10 years old and needed some help gaining control of the clutter in her bedroom. I knew the family very well and spent a lot of time in most areas of their home.

"Ugh! My daughter's bedroom is never clean," Jamie lamented.

"She has too much stuff," I said. Remember me? Always direct and to the point. Especially with my friends.

"Yes! Her horses are out of control! She leaves them out on the floor and they get in the way!"

"Let me see this room," I offered.

Yes, just as I thought. The room *was* full. Full of "gifts" for the child. It was busting at the seams with over 100 stuffed animals, heirloom items that had been passed down, and so much more. And there on the floor were the horses.

"Where do the horses go when they are not being played with?"

"In a box in the closet, but they are *always* being played with."

Hmmm. The answer was obvious to me. She should keep the horses and box up the museum. But how?

"I tell you what," I said. "I will organize your daughter's room *with* her and *without* you on two conditions."

"First, she can box up anything she is not using. Not get rid of it, but box it up to make space for what she wants to play with and have on display in her room."

The color drained from Jamie's face, "Okay...." I could tell she was bracing for number two.

"And, second, I will need shelving in the closet. Just against the side wall, 2 ½ feet wide and about 5 feet high."

"We can do that," she said, "But I want to stay and help."

"Nope, no way. If you are anywhere close by, your daughter will not be honest with me. She won't feel free to box up the gifts you and your mom have given her in order to make room for the horses."

"But we want the horses in the closet and the gifts out," she pleaded.

"I know," I sympathized, "But her room will never stay organized if there are not spaces for her own passion projects. You have to choose: do you want it to be and stay organized, or do you want her room to be decorated the way you prefer?"

"Both," she laughed.

And then I said it. "I promise if you let me and your daughter work together alone, once I get her organized, it will *stay* organized."

"I know you're right; let me know when you are done."

I had so much fun! Plus, I was right…her room did stay organized throughout that phase of her life.

I was discovering that I was successful as a professional organizer and my clients were able to maintain the organization over time because I was teaching them the *skills* of organization.

Clutter Comfort Levels

My phone rang again. "Lisa! Help! I don't know what to do! My house is a wreck, and I can't get on top of it again! We have to start over!"

Now I was in a full panic. This was my second loyal client from the spring; one of the only two clients I worked with on a regular basis. They were the two clients I had taken through the "mommy makeover." When I left them in June, their laundry rooms, personal closets, and kitchens were decluttered and organized.

Had summer erased all my work? Were my solutions too hard to maintain? Was organization really a thing you had to do every season?

I needed to find out…and fast!

Luckily, these two clients lived within a few miles of each other. I scheduled a free one hour consultation with each of them the next day to find out what went wrong.

"Lisa, look at this office; it's a wreck! I can't find anything and my business is so behind!" Sheryl moaned.

Before I could make a comment, she was on her way to the basement. "And this! There are toys all over the place! I am stepping on Legos everywhere. Just wait until you see my storage room. It's even worse!"

Oh. My. Goodness! This storage room was half the size of the house. Treasures, memories, decorations, clothing, gifts, kid's toys, sporting equipment, and more lined the walls, hung from the ceiling, and were piled waist high as far as the eye could see. There was a lot of work to do.

"Sheryl, what about the spaces we did last time? The laundry room, your closet and the kitchen? Can I see those spaces?"

"Sure," she said, "but those are fine."

A-ha! Hallelujah!

The scene played out almost exactly the same way at Jenny's house. The spaces we had already worked on together were fine; it was the rest of the house that needed the work.

The relief I felt was immense. I was surely onto something. Both of these women were diagnosed with ADHD; they had yet to experience success with any organizational plan or professional organizer. The systems that we put in place *were* working, *were* maintained, and their spouses had noticed, too. I scheduled twice monthly sessions with each of them, and over the course of that year got both houses completely organized. It did not happen overnight, but it did happen.

This was a lot like what happened when I faced my kids' linen closet. I needed to address both the *stuff* in the space and the *habits* surrounding the way the space was being used. I needed to figure out what to remove from the space, but I also needed to think about what to *add* to the space. I had learned many mental skills of organization prior to tackling the kids' bathroom and linen closet, and I was able to apply them there. The process of thinking about how to organize a space is what I call the mindset of organization.

Once you gain an organizational mindset, it can be hard to tolerate your old way of thinking. Newly organized spaces where you used to tolerate clutter become more visible and more annoying if they start to become disorganized again. Once you get one space under control and maintainable, then you start to notice other areas that need your focus, too. You can no longer tolerate the same level of chaos and volume of stuff. Your brain actually resets.

These clients got started on their organization, and now they were ready to tackle the rest of the house. They had learned the skills of organizing, they had changed their mindsets, and had taken the next step knowing they could maintain their progress. Progress over perfection!

I was noticing that my spaces in my own home were staying organized, too. All the decluttering and organizing that I had completed in the spring had led to sustainable systems. As I revisited each space, I was able to declutter and reorganize in a fraction of the time. Some spaces I could skip entirely; others areas, such as my closet, still needed more work. I was doing some maintenance and resetting, but I never had to do the *major* decluttering again.

I did have to revisit different areas in my home periodically. I think this is where people think they have "fallen off the wagon"–when one area starts to get out of hand. Why do we have this expectation for home organization? Do you clean your house once and expect it to stay that way? I wish! That's not how it works at my house. Are you able to just shop for clothes once? Of course not! Changing seasons, sizes, and occasions dictate that these are things that you must attend to on a relatively regular basis. There are so many similar tasks that are not on our radar until it is evident that there is an immediate need. My family, business, and personal needs have continued to change over time. The key to *staying* organized is putting some time into regular maintenance as your life changes. One big change for me, though, is that I now don't dread walking into my closet and trying to find something to wear. That first year, I spent a lot of time on my wardrobe.

Leveling Up My Wardrobe on a Budget

Six months had passed since the first time I attempted to organize my closet. Throughout the summer, I continued to happily discard items that didn't fit or were hopelessly ruined. I did get a few more wearings out of some of my favorites pieces by acting surprised and remarking that a stain "had just happened today." Don't tell me you haven't done that, too!

Much to my chagrin, there was now very little to declutter… and even less to actually wear. As I took stock of my wardrobe for the first time, I realized that while organizing often started with decluttering, sometimes you actually needed to add items.

What did an organized closet look like?

I had organized a dozen professional women's closets in the past year. I understood the desire to have a beautiful, rainbow-organized closet, but even my clients with tens of thousands of dollars' worth of clothes did not achieve the perfect photo-worthy closet.

In one client's closet, I had built a shoe wall connecting laminate shoe organizers from the floor to the ceiling. Even that was not enough to house the hundreds of shoes I found in the unfinished basement, guest bedroom, under the bed, and in the primary closet. For some women, shoes are both a necessity and a passion project all rolled into one.

I looked at my fourteen pairs of shoes and thought, "How many more did I need?" I really wasn't sure.

The same client had a beautiful collection of handbags that ranged from the functional TJ MAXX finds to very expensive gifts. I enjoyed stuffing and arranging those handbags at the top of her closet, matching in color the clothing hung below, giving the closet and its contents a perfectly coordinated look.

I had 2 handbags. No organization necessary.

Then there were the clothes. This client had more than she could ever wear. Brand new items with tags still attached were crowded next to her favorites.

I felt like Goldilocks. By day, I helped women who had too much, and at night in my own closet, I had too little. How could I get a "just right" amount of clothes?

It would be years before I would shop in a traditional store again. Our family budget priorities put my wardrobe at the bottom of the list. I was fine with that, except that my clothes were literally falling apart.

My next closet client cleared out ten black garbage bags of clothes from her closet. These were nice clothes from Talbots, White House Black Market, and a variety of department stores; they were all set to be discarded. By now, I was offering to drop off donations at Goodwill for my clients and mail them the donation ticket. Nancy told me, "Keep whatever you want before you make the donations." I never would have taken things without the client's permission, but I was so grateful for her generosity.

That night, I brought *all* of the bags in my house and went through each one. I kept six sweaters and a few tops. Nine and a half bags went to Goodwill the next day.

Honestly, it feels weird telling you this. Many clients have gifted me items over the years. Our family has been the recipient of all kinds of charity in our lifetime. In our early married years and as I write today, we have been able to bless others with our own donations. In 2012, though, I was a recipient. I think every life has different seasons, and we learn from both the giving *and* the receiving.

What makes a good wardrobe, anyway? Sometimes hand-me-downs from friends or family members are simply what you have. It's hard to know exactly what you will need personally, and even harder to anticipate the needs of a child.

While we were waiting to adopt our babies, I was obsessed with preparing for their arrival. I had researched exactly what I needed to have on hand and how many items of clothing a baby needs in each size.

Ah, youthful naivete. As an infant, Joey had horrible reflux and went through twenty burp cloths and four to five pairs of pajamas a day, every day. So much for an ideal wardrobe list!

Then there was the year Joey grew out of his pants every four months. He went from a 3T to a size 6x in about 12 months. Hello growth spurt! Buying four or five pairs of jeans at a time was SO expensive! I thought I was brilliant when I bought four pairs of size 7 and 8 jeans on sale. It would be two more years before Joey wore a size 7, and when they finally did fit, he was naturally in a season in which he would only wear sweatpants. Of course!

While my early attempts to predict how many clothes my kids would need failed, I was learning. With each season and size, I was more prudent about what I purchased. I had a minimum threshold in each size of the basics: pajamas, pants, shirts, sweaters, and sweatshirts.

Unfortunately, the basics are not as much fun for grandparents to buy as are the holiday-themed sweaters and little special occasion outfits. I was left with a dozen beautiful and never-worn dresses for Abby, all gifts with price tags that would have funded a year of the basics that she actually needed. Sometimes I just let her wear the dressy clothes without saving them for a "special" occasion. Who doesn't love dressing a precious little girl? You can't tell grandparents, "No, please don't buy that beautiful pink dress. She needs sweatpants." At least I couldn't.

Too many dressy clothes and not enough of the basics. This was true in my wardrobe, as well. Don't we all love buying those statement necklaces and party dresses? Women are willing to pay top dollar for beautiful things. Once you hit a certain age, though, you long for simple things like a pair of black pants that really fit. It takes time and effort to find good, basic clothes that we can wear every day.

For my closet to feel organized, I didn't need an overabundance of pieces that I wouldn't wear. I needed to figure out what I should have on hand in order to get dressed every morning.

I needed more clothes. My determination of need was that I only had five outfits in my closet. Not having at least seven to ten choices was too confining for me. I didn't have the financial resources for new clothing–even at Target–so I went to my local resale shop. I purchased 13 items for less than $100.

Being able to buy brand name clothes for less than $10 per item fit both my budget and my style. Over the next few years, I built my wardrobe up with second-hand clothing that looked and felt great. I stayed on a budget that was right for my family, but it took time. In resale shops, you never know what you will find, and you will encounter more than one amazing deal that you need to leave in the store. Just because it costs only a few dollars does not mean that you need to bring it home! That's how some women find their closets suddenly out of hand—from too many good deals. I still needed to find a few things while being cautious of the lure of the good deals.

Investing a little in my wardrobe every few months, I bought only what fit my current weight and looked great on me at that point in my life. I did not buy anything for "someday" or "maybe if I" because I was focused on my reality. I enjoyed my trips to the resale shop and tried on each item before buying.

Nothing came home that I didn't think I would wear at least 20 times.

It was in this season that I was discovering my style. Instead of lamenting that I couldn't replicate my young adult shopping sprees with mom, I was embracing what I *could* do. Being able to buy nice clothes at such great discounts, I played around with different styles each season to find what was authentically me. It turns out I love to wear boot cut jeans with Dansko shoes, or skinny jeans with high heels. My favorite theme for my upper body is to keep me warm! Zip up jackets or blazers that cinch at the waist accentuate the better part of my curves.

A nice perk to my new shopping plan was that since my entire outfit on any given day cost a total of only around $25, it didn't matter if I wore it on an organizing job or to a school meeting. Even though my clothing budget was small, my professional look improved, and along with it, my confidence grew.

Today, my motto for myself and my kids is that if we own it, we wear it. I do not "save" items to wear for a fancy event or a special occasion. If it is in my closet, it is fair game!

It turns out that we need a lot less clothing than we think. It is an awesome feeling to walk in your closet and know that everything fits and that you enjoy wearing it. I was trying to create how I thought an organized closet would look. It turns out being organized is a *feeling*.

And I was really starting to feel organized!

I Am a Functional Organizer

October is one of the most productive months of the year for so many Americans. The cooler fall air and the personal rejuvenation from summer both serve to fuel a more focused and productive fall energy.

By October, I had found my professional organization groove and clients were ready to work with me to get their homes organized! I had replaced my teacher salary and finally felt that I could breathe a little easier.

October was the month when I realized this was going to work! It had taken nine months, but I had finally made the full transition into a working-from-home mom with an income that would grow; I was proud to partner with Greg to sustain our family financially.

I was also growing in my organizational confidence in other areas. It turns out some of the organizational ideas I had thought were true, were actually not…the biggest of these being about containers.

Organization is Not About Cute Containers

I'm not going to lie. I *really* wanted this to be true. I **love** cute containers!

Years ago, I spent a good portion of the summer organizing the kids' playroom. I bought matching red bins and three short bookshelves to create a Pottery Barn looking play area.

The bins looked amazing on the shelves and the playroom looked great until the kids actually used it. Toys in use were often left out and only put back in their red bins when I decided "enough is enough" and cleaned up the area myself.

Over time, the playroom kept looking better and better, but not because the kids learned the system. It was because they stopped playing with the toys! They would search for and retrieve their favorites, but in those solid red canvas bins, they couldn't see what they had and forgot it existed. Try as I might, the cute picture-perfect playroom never functioned well for me or my kids.

So what *does* work?

Think about a daycare or kindergarten classroom. Open shelving, clear containers, and pictures that show you where each toy lives. That works.

I mean, I should have known that, right? I am an early childhood teacher. I designed daycare centers. I have taught four, five, and six year olds. My classrooms were very organized and fun. At home, with my "mom hat" on, for some reason, I wanted to have a space that looked like a sales catalog. Why?

What is this hold that Pinterest, catalogs and magazines have on us?

After nine months of decluttering and organizing, my storage room was overflowing with bins of all sizes and shapes that I had emptied as I organized my house. At first, I kept them all. They were "good bins" and I paid good money for them, right? It took me another year before I was ready to get rid of most of them.

There is nothing like the feeling of bringing home a car full of bins and transforming a bookshelf, closet, or room into a picture-perfect image. I still have the desire to do that today. I know now, that that is called decorating, not organizing. No matter how hard you try, you just can't decorate clutter and expect transformation.

Organizing is the process of putting like items together in a place that makes sense. Organizing solves the problem of determining where an item lives. Decorating makes your space look pretty.

Understanding the Organizing Cycle

This led me to my next realization. I am *not* a decorator.

A wise coach once told me you should know where your clients are coming from and where they will go after you. I cannot and should not solve all of your household challenges.

Often people find me after they have started decluttering. Other times, the organization that worked for clients in one phase of their life is not working in the next phase. Most of my clients are not new to organizing, but they want to develop stronger organizational skills. Sometimes, they even become a professional organizer and share their own knowledge and experience with others.

As I organized my own home and taught others the skills of organization, I have identified three stages of organization. These apply to *anything* you are organizing including your home, your paper, or even your calendar. First, **declutter**. Decluttering is removing things you no longer need or want. Second, **organize**. Organizing is putting similar things together and establishing a designated space or container for those things. Third, **increase productivity**. Increasing productivity is the act of getting more done in less time by identifying tools and techniques that make you more efficient. Sometimes, this involves developing habits and creating systems. Once these three stages are complete, *then* it makes sense to decorate, to make things pretty, and to focus on the visual aesthetic.

I am an expert in the organizing stage of the cycle. I can help you finish decluttering and move on to organizing. This was the hardest, yet most freeing idea that I have fully embraced–I didn't need to have all of the answers to all of the questions! I love the community that surrounds Organize 365, and I love speaking into the lives of women. As my clients and now the Organize 365 online community get organized, they want me to be a business coach, a decorator, and their digital organization solution, as well. They have connected with me, they trust my teaching, and they want me to help them continue their transformation.

My response is always the same–no, thank you. Not because I can't, but because I shouldn't. I believe that I will make a bigger impact on more people if I stay focused on organization at home. This book is launching along with the first of many research studies Organize 365 will undertake to identify, describe, and bring light to the state of housework in the American home.

How do you even define housework? In our research, we realized that no one ever has provided a definition. Mind. Blown. It is actually four categories of tasks rolled into one word. We need better definitions, more words to describe those four categories, and solid data to know where we are starting so that we can measure our progress. Building a vocabulary and researching this traditionally female role are vital to communicating what women contribute to the home.

While we want the gender equity that we see growing in society and workplaces to also be observed in homes, it is not there yet. There is a lot of interest in this part of the discussion. Organize 365 is starting the research, but there is so much more to explore.

As an educator, much of my focus was on those who are diagnosed with ADHD. We have so many great strategies and supports for this community at work and school, but none at home. Adult women struggle with home organization the most. I know my work and collaboration with others can change that in the next decade.

I am a business coach. I can digitize your files and lists, but so can so many others. To be honest, they will probably coach and digitize you better than I could. So I bless and release my clients to go find their next teacher.

Organize 365 is there to help you get your home, paper, and work organized. We want you to pursue *your* unique purpose in this life. I am doubling down on teaching the skill of organizing and developing the curriculum and supports needed for my clients in their home classrooms all over the world. I love being a teacher!

Projects in Purgatory

As my home organization took hold and there was less clutter in the living spaces of our home, I was left with random papers, clippings, files, supplies, books, computer files, and boxes of other papers.

At first, I kept consolidating these items and piles into the storage areas of my home. We all have that space or spaces where we put things, "just in case." I like to call that your Hot Mess Room. The Hot Mess Room can be a basement storage area, shed, attic, spare bedroom, paid storage space, or even a hallway. We all have one, or sometimes many, of these spaces.

As my home became more organized, these spaces grew larger and more daunting. The problem was that these piles were not items to be organized... they were ideas. They were physical representations of passions, projects, and future ideas not yet realized.

By the time I got to this mountain of dreams, most were long since forgotten, and I lacked the passion, desire, and enthusiasm to ever complete them. But the money was already spent and there was my conundrum. Do I finish a project just because I paid for the materials...simply to be able to check it off the to-do list? Or do I part with the supplies and call it a loss?

Another lesson learned: I am an idea person. I have too many ideas.

As painful as it was, I let almost all these projects go, and to prevent this feeling of regret from recurring, I created the 24 Hour Rule.

The 24 Hour Rule

I love to explore different personality frameworks. One that I have found particularly useful is called the Kolbe. It looks at the way you prefer to approach projects and take action. On the Kolbe scale (kolbe.com), I am a quick start. As soon as I get an idea, I'm ready to go. I jump in and get started, preferably right now. I do not research, or ponder, or otherwise prepare.

I am really good at the idea phase, which includes buying the stuff to get started. I run out of time and energy in the doing phase, and rarely get to the enjoying phase of the cycle. I see a recipe, and I save it. Sometimes, I even buy the ingredients! I rarely put it on the dinner menu and actually make the dish. I want new curtains, I buy them, but I never hang them up. I see a cute craft at the store, I buy the material, but I never make the craft. I do; however, have to store those supplies for all of the unfinished projects.

As I cleared through the backlog during my decluttering session, I decided I needed a new rule. I called it the 24 Hour Rule.

The "24 Hour Rule" is a rule I impose upon myself. When I find a great idea, I ask myself "Can I do this within 24 hours?" If an idea is *that* good, I take action on it within 24 hours. I no longer buy, print, or save things–unless I am going to take action on them within the next 24 hours.

Following this rule has allowed me to reduce guilt and to give myself permission to let go of things that are good ideas that are not actually going to get done. This has helped me to avoid or delay unnecessary purchases and to stop adding new obligations and expectations to my time and energy. I also do not have to store, save, or shuffle around a pile of recipes that looked good in the moment.

For books, I am even stricter with this rule. With immediate electronic delivery through so many different reading apps, I have to be ready to start reading a book right now before I purchase it. When I am ready to read, I buy the electronic book and start reading. Oddly enough, I do not put pressure on myself to finish books. For me, buying books is the least expensive way to educate myself. I am willing to risk not loving something – as long as I start reading. Not every book expectation matches up to reality, and I'm ok with that. My bigger concern is avoiding a pile of books I wanted to read and paid for that no longer interest me. Every reader I know has a stack of books for someday, and with the popularity of various e-reader devices and apps, those stacks are still there, only now they're online. Electronic clutter is still clutter. That list of books you downloaded to be read someday can cause the same guilt as the physical shelves of books you need to declutter. I don't have time for that, and you don't, either! I also prefer to spend my money on books I want to read *right now* instead of books I wanted to read in the past.

Ask yourself: Can I take action on this item, this idea, this project, this recipe, or this book, within the next 24 hours? If the answer is no, then don't purchase the items related to that project.

More Systems and Rules

As an adult homeowner, I like that I am in charge of making the rules. I had been waiting my whole life to "be on my own" and make my own rules like I pretended to do when playing "Big Friend" with my sister. What I actually did, though, was make no rules…at least until I learned that rules are as important for adults as they were for my preschool students. Rules give us structure and boundaries, as well as reduce the amount of mental gymnastics it requires to make decisions.

Creating rules like the 24 Hour Rule allowed me to purchase and start projects with excitement and not from a posture of scarcity or just because an item was on sale. To be honest, I still bought sale items and searched for the best price on project supplies, but seeing a sale was no longer the primary reason I started a project or made a purchase. Even if I paid a little more when I was ready to do a project in the next 24 hours, I saved significantly more by *not* buying the parts for nine other projects that I would never start or finish.

Once the 24 Hour Rule was in place, I only had one question to ask when starting something new. Could I actually get started in 24 hours? If yes, then game on!

As I saw how effective the 24 Hour Rule was in my life, I created some more rules for myself.

The Sunday Basket® System Rule is that if something (mail, to-do, task, bill, etc.) can wait until Sunday, it must wait until Sunday. This habit of delaying household decisions until one day of the week has saved me so much time on a daily basis. Deferring things allows me to make better decisions with our time and resources when I look at a whole week's worth of planning at one scheduled time.

Lisa's Breakfast Rule has been going strong for the last nine years. I am not a person who needs to have a lot of variety in my meals. Eating the same breakfast for almost a decade has freed up my mind, simplified my grocery shopping, and kept me going until mid morning every day. Each morning, I make a Keurig K cup of caramel coffee with one teaspoon of raw sugar and milk. I grab a Zone Perfect peanut butter chocolate protein bar and that's it. No decisions need to be made. I just follow the rule. The rules don't have to be complicated to be extremely effective.

The Laundry Rule is that I only do laundry on the weekend. I do the laundry anytime from Friday night to Sunday night. This rule allows me to go about my week without thinking about the laundry. I can lay out my outfits for the week, everything is clean at one time, and I know exactly when I will wash clothes again. It's not a surprise. It's routine. Routines smooth out the wrinkles in my life, and they can do the same for you.

To make this rule work, I invested in more socks and underwear for each family member and showed the kids how to do laundry. There is the rare occasion where laundry gets done on a weekday—but it is the exception, not the rule.

Errand Day is always on Tuesday. After completing my Sunday Basket® routine, I load the car up with any returns, drop-offs, or errand notes on Sunday afternoon or evening. On Tuesday, I run all of my errands. Having only one weekly errand day has saved us so much money by eliminating spontaneous impulse buys and "quick trips" to the store. I know what stops I need to make, I know what order to make them in, and if someone asks me to drop off or pick up something, I know that I can fit it in on Tuesday.

These rules and more have all saved me time and money. Once you realize the power of rules, you may be tempted to create dozens; however, that isn't really necessary. Five to ten well-planned rules will save your sanity and your decision-making power for what truly matters to you most.

Growth & Grace

Ironically, organizing the holidays has more to do with planning and mental preparation than organizing physical supplies.

What?! I know it doesn't seem that way, but hang in there for a minute. This revelation was a huge game-changer for me and allowed me to fully step into this next season of life with my family.

So much of what happens at the holidays is based on the past. Past traditions. Family expectations. Religious observances. We often carry subconscious expectations about what is "necessary" to celebrate a particular holiday. Sometimes those traditions are based on wonderful memories and are completely doable. Sometimes, what we feel we are expected or required to do can be a burden. Oh, I know you heard me there.

As I approached the upcoming 2012 holidays with my middle school age kids, I worried about changing anything we had done in the past and wondered if changes would "ruin their holidays." That mama guilt can be a sneaky thing! I hadn't even changed anything yet, and I was already feeling guilty.

Many of our fun family traditions abruptly ended when our family experienced unexpected changes that were beyond my control. A decade earlier, my parents divorced. Five years later, my father passed away, and Greg's sister had just moved away; we found our holidays changing again. We survived all of those changes, but now I was thinking about doing things differently on purpose.

So, I started by asking myself–What did I want to do this holiday season?

So often, I find myself modifying my plans and continuing on familiar pathways without stopping and thinking about what I truly want. Our holiday celebrations had shifted to become an awkward patching together of what was left of our old family traditions.

Add to that the fact that even though I was a grown woman, I didn't feel I could make any holiday changes. In my mind, it was my family who broke the happy holidays. There was no longer a childhood home to visit. The once large, inter-twined families of my mother and father no longer celebrated together because of their divorce. It seemed like we just had the memories of the happy holidays.

Greg's family holiday traditions were left intact until his sister moved away and his stepfather passed away. Today, only our family and Greg's mother live in the Cincinnati area. This is our holiday family now.

Planning for the holidays can be heavy for so many reasons.

There are lots of feelings and emotions about what was, what "should" be, and what could possibly be in the future. The year 2020 taught us that nothing stays the same, and that even the strongest traditions eventually change. For some, the holidays are reminders of loved ones lost, dreams not achieved, and other emotionally difficult experiences.

In addition to losing my storybook holiday experience, I am NOT a cook. I couldn't even make up for anything we were lacking with a delicious holiday feast! With each passing year, this weakness is more apparent and feels like a huge family disappointment for me.

I did not have the desire to, nor was I capable of becoming a fabulous cook overnight. I needed to focus on what I could control to recreate our holiday traditions for this year and the years to come.

Meaningful Holiday Memories

It was my year of transformation, so, as with everything else that I do, I started with thinking and research. In particular, I started with a family survey. No, not the paper and pencil kind, although I did have a list. I started by asking pointed questions at family dinner and writing down the family's responses.

What are your favorite Thanksgiving foods?
What is your favorite Thanksgiving dessert?
What are your favorite appetizers?
What are your favorite Christmas foods?
What do you like to eat at home on winter break?
What do you look forward to at Christmas time?
What is your favorite holiday tradition?

I quickly realized that many of the foods that I thought were essential were not even included in the responses to my survey. The key to using this survey tactic with your family is to ask the questions early in November. Before the hustle and bustle of the holidays are in full swing, you will hear about the things that they are looking forward to the most. This is really fun research, but get ready to be surprised! In addition, and I can't stress this enough, decide before you begin to not be offended by what is included or excluded in your family's lists of the favorites. The point is to focus on the must-haves, and not to stew over the time, money, and effort that you used to spend on things that were as not important to your family.

I love pumpkin pie. I cannot get enough! Through my official Woodruff Holiday Survey, I found out that both of my kids also love pumpkin pie. That year I bought a pumpkin pie every week from a local bakery, and we ate like kings! I may not be the best cook, but adding pumpkin pie to our November and December meals really makes the holidays come to life for our family.

Ironically, even if daily dinners are not my forte, I can make a great Thanksgiving feast. I have about 5 dinners I can make with all the sides, and Thanksgiving is one of them. I like cooking all day, and the food is delicious! In response to my holiday survey, Greg mentioned that he loved Thanksgiving leftovers. At the time, my mother-in-law was still in charge of the big feast for our family, but we never had leftovers in our house since we weren't hosting the meal. Why can't we have Thanksgiving dinner more than once?!

I cooked a full Thanksgiving dinner 3 times that year in December, January, and February. We even made homemade turkey vegetable soup in the crockpot—another special request from Greg. I practiced giving myself grace and making the decisions that best supported what my family found most meaningful and most important.

While I have mostly focused on holiday traditions involving food, I was surprised by the things my kids remembered as traditions that I didn't actually do on purpose. I was grateful to learn that several of the most time-consuming and laborious tasks were not that important to my family, after all. Just listen and see what your family anticipates the most. You can still do a few special things for your own holiday celebration—just know that you don't have to go all out if no one else cares.

Taking the Hustle Out of the Holiday Bustle

When I thought about what *I* wanted during the holiday season, one major item on my list was to be better prepared and not shopping constantly. I felt like I spent so much of the holidays in stores. I set out to change that this year.

Why was I in the stores so much? Here are the many reasons:

- Gift buying
- Regular food shopping
- Holiday food shopping
- Holiday baking shopping
- Small crafts for kids before Christmas
- Food to take to holiday parties
- Fun, snacky foods to eat at home between meals
- Cold and flu medicines, even if just in case
- Extra cards, gifts, cash

I decided to try an experiment. I thought through every single thing that was on my calendar from November 10–January 4. In addition to my regular holiday shopping list, I followed up with a massive grocery shopping list.

I knew the bill would be large, but could I take a day, shop it all and be home the month of December? I thought it was worth trying.

Not having the cash up front for my massive shopping trip, I swiped our credit card through the machine and broke out in a cold sweat. I had two overflowing grocery carts full of holiday food and supplies. I was transported back to my shopping trip from last January, but this time I had a plan. All of these items were needed, would be used, and had a place to go when I got home.

Best. Decision. Ever!

Oh my goodness, I cannot state this enough. Taking a day in November to purchase as much of your baking, cooking and household needs at once was so freeing for me! Even though the bill was high, we saved so much money and time that year. Just avoiding the impulse buys that inevitably come with multiple grocery trips was a major budget relief.

The ability to make dinner, appetizers, snacks, or cookies without skipping a beat was amazing! I was prepared for anything!

The next year, I added holiday paper plates to my shopping list. We ate on the "good china" when company came over to visit, but, when it was just our family, we used the disposable plates and saved more time with meal prep and clean up.

I wasn't cooking from scratch, but hot out of the oven pop & bake cinnamon rolls, bakery-bought pumpkin pie, and our favorite holiday beef log made it feel like the holidays. I may not be a cook, but I'll share this recipe with you. Remember, I love appetizers! This is one of my favorites.

Grandma's Beef Log Recipe

Ingredients:

8 oz. cream cheese
1/4 c. parmesan cheese
1 t. horseradish
1/3 c. chopped olives
1 c. diced dried beef

Blend the cream cheese, parmesan cheese and horseradish.

Stir in the olives.

Shape into two rolls.

Roll each in the diced dried beef.

Refrigerate until time to serve with crackers! My favorite crackers with this beef log are Triscuts.

Appetizers! That was my number one answer to the holiday survey! Yum! I also wanted our home to feel fun and holiday-ish. I want our kids to have good holiday memories that would last a lifetime.

Creating 3 Sunday Baskets®:
Holiday, New Year, and Regular Sunday Basket®

Now that I had the supplies we needed, I realized that I needed a way to simplify all that I had left to do in the last six weeks of the year. I found myself making too many lists and becoming overwhelmed with all the moving parts.

Even the veteran planners among us have our planning prowess put to the test the last six weeks of the year. I found myself spending too much time making my lists and checking them twice. My focus was scattered, and I had little time to actually *do* those important tasks. My Sunday Basket® planning time turned into marathon sessions ending in long to-do lists each week. I needed a better system.

I again applied those analytical skills and questioning tactics. Here's what I learned: by mid-November, I have three kinds of tasks. First, the regular, weekly household Sunday Basket® tasks. Second, there are the holiday tasks. Third, I have my ideas for the upcoming new year. I decided to create three boxes of tasks to match these categories for my Sunday Basket® planning time. I immediately gained more time and was able to compartmentalize my tasks even more. I could now tackle each box as my time and energy allowed.

The reality is that my weekly Sunday Basket® tasks were urgent and important; they were vital to keeping my home standing and my family thriving. I needed to continue to set aside time each and every week to work on these tasks. However, by removing the holiday and New Year tasks, my Sunday Basket® felt so much lighter and I was able to work through it much more quickly.

I decided to dedicate a separate Sunday Basket® as my "holiday basket." Everything related to our holiday plans, recipes, gift receipts and even some small gifts were tucked safely inside. I could drop small gift items inside, and I had a place to keep track of all of the holiday tasks without clogging up my brain or organization for my general household functioning. The Holiday box contained tasks that were important but not vital to the health and safety of my family. Plus, this basket is active for only a few short weeks, and can then be stored until next year.

Finally, I set up my "New Year" Sunday Basket®. The New Year basket was for anything that I would not need until January 1st or later. As I put slash pockets, notes, and projects in this basket, I looked forward to creating a New Year processing and planning day the week between Christmas and the first day of the new year. The New Year box gave me a place to dream and hold ideas that I knew I wouldn't have the time or energy for during the last six weeks of the year. Keeping them in a separate box meant that they did not waste my attention and concentration on items that could be deferred to a later date.

My Sunday Basket® sessions on Sunday were still longer than normal because of the business of November and December.

However, having the New Year basket to defer tasks to, and quickly running through *only* the necessary Sunday Basket® weekly tasks, was far more efficient. This left me time to focus on and organize the holiday tasks without distraction from the other two boxes.

Honing this system over the years has made the end of the year function almost as smoothly as the rest of the year. Surprising, I know! It didn't happen overnight, but every year, I get better at my own process, and I'm proud of how much less stressed the holidays are for my family as a result. This year could be your year to join me in de-stressing the holidays! Each fall, Organize 365 offers a *free* Holiday Blitz to help you plan and organize your own November and December holiday season. You can find it in our newsletter or on social media heading into the holidays.

Making New Memories

Thanksgiving has never been my favorite holiday. I love seeing extended family, but food alone is not my thing. For me, Christmas is where the magic is… or was.

As a teacher, I would always have the day off on the Wednesday before Thanksgiving. I always chose to use that day to decorate for the holidays. Greg would come home at the end of the day and walk into a winter wonderland.

Our weekend would be full of family and friends at others' homes, while coming home to Christmas cookies, cinnamon candles, and lots of Christmas lights at ours.

Somewhere in the last 10 years, I went from looking forward to Chritstmas to dreading it. How does that happen? It took me a while to figure it out.

As a child, I remember my grandmother coming down to our house and spending the whole day with my mom lavishly decorating every nook and cranny for the holidays. My mother is an artist and would often add new decorations each year. What's more, she always included fresh flowers and greenery in her displays—so beautiful! They were magical, and I looked forward to one day having my own house to spend the day decorating for the holidays. I think I expected it to look just like Grandma and Mom did it all those years ago

Once Greg and I married, I decorated our home for every single holiday. I was a teacher, and I treated our home just like a classroom. I enjoyed adding seasonal decor that I purchased at craft shows to our collection. Every year, Greg bought me a new snowman for the collection I put up in January when the Christmas decorations came down.

By the time our kids were in kindergarten and first grade, decorating was starting to feel more like a chore. That year, even with all of the changes I was making in our home, I just didn't want to do it. At all. What was the matter with me? I had made so much progress. This was to be the culminating event of my long productive year!

I decided to take a day off from organizing while the kids were still in school and decorate the house alone. A Lisa Day.

In the past, this would have made my heart sing. Decorating had always been a passion project of mine. This year, I found myself crying on the floor. I made it through putting up the nativity, wreaths, stockings, and mantel decorations, but I just couldn't decorate the tree.

Exploring New Christmas Decoration Ideas

My mother started an awesome Christmas tradition when I was a baby. Every year, she and some of my family members would give me a Christmas tree ornament. Then when I left home, I had a full tree's worth of ornaments to decorate my own Christmas tree.

Many of the ornaments in my collection were handmade, personalized, and specific to my passions or family activities for the year they were given to me. When Greg and I got married, even though it was in August, I followed my mom's tradition and gave my bridesmaids each a Christmas ornament to remember the occasion.

Christmas ornaments were a minor hobby of mine. Greg and I collected ornaments when we went on vacation and bought them for each other and our kids. My Christmas tree is full of family memories.

And that year, it was just too much. Too many memories. Holiday traditions and memories from years ago. People who had passed. Future dreams left unrealized. It was all so heavy. I could *not* find my usual holiday spirit.

As luck would have it, one of my regular organizing clients was getting ready to move. She was decluttering every inch of her home, including her fun matching peppermint and snowman tree decorations. She kindly gifted them to me. I decorated our tree with her decorations that year. I felt lighter and more hopeful as I trimmed our tree with those non-sentimental, completely adorable ornaments.

Christmas Cards

The weight of past Christmases didn't end with the tree. There was also the Christmas card to prepare. I love to receive Christmas cards, read annual Christmas letters, and pore over family photos. It is one of the highlights of the season for me.

The last few years we had stopped sending Christmas cards and an annual letter. I told Greg it was because we couldn't afford it, which was kind of true. It does cost $100 or more to send a Christmas card to all of our family and friends, but that wasn't my main reason.

First, we didn't have a family photo. More importantly, I didn't have what I thought was enough content for a Christmas letter. Our family was very blessed with our annual trip to the beach to see Greg's family, a good education for our kids, a warm home, and good medical care. We had more than others and felt extremely grateful.

In my head, Christmas letters aren't meant to repeat those sentiments year after year. They're supposed to trumpet new achievements, promotions, and accolades while highlighting amazing vacation photos. Making a Christmas card during that season of life left me with a feeling of lack, instead of the gratefulness I feel during the rest of the year.

For that reason, we still do not send a Christmas card, although I truly treasure every one I receive. I'm so proud of what we have been able to accomplish as a family, but I don't like how preparing that letter can leave me suddenly thinking in a comparative way toward others. So I don't do it. It's okay if you do. I do enjoy reading the ones that come my way each Christmas.

As you process through the items you have saved for the holidays, you may also stir up emotional feelings from the past. It took me a long time to realize that these simple holiday traditions were changing my mood so dramatically.

I prided myself on being a giver, willing to help and offer support when others need it. That Christmas, I realized the power of receiving. Receiving used Christmas ornaments unlocked the magic of my Christmas spirit and the wonder of a Christmas tree again. Be open to receiving; you might be surprised at the gifts that come your way.

Simplifying Christmas Cookies

Another fun holiday memory from my childhood was traveling up to my Grandmother's house for a full day of baking Christmas cookies. My grandmother was an amazing baker, and by the end of the day, her house would be filled with dozens of varieties of cookies—each one finished to a melt in your mouth level of perfection.

While this tradition of starting from scratch was vivid in my mind, only the final steps of decorating (and eating!) sugar cookies was the memory my kids held tightly. The kids didn't care about fancy cookies or having such a wide variety. I realized that they did not help me bake or even watch me when I made the sugar cookies. They just wanted to be able to decorate them.

I didn't have a lot of time or desire to bake cookies that year, and I realized that I could roll out the "slice and bake" sugar cookies from the refrigerated section at the grocery store. The following year, I realized the kids didn't even care about sugar cookie shapes! They truly just wanted to decorate the cookies, so I sliced circle cookies and baked them. This was so much easier for me and it was what they really wanted, too.

This past year, my kids confessed that they like chocolate chip cookies the best. Chocolate chip cookies are not Christmas cookies to me, but they are the cookies my kids like the best. So that is what we made. Slice and bake chocolate chip cookies were in my oven every week for the last 4 weeks of the year. My kids were in heaven!

I am the queen of making things more complicated than they need to be. With age, I have really started to ask myself first, before starting something new, what do I want to accomplish? In December, I want a decorated tree, warm cookies, and to enjoy the Christmas cards we receive. Decluttering emotional memories and unrealistic expectations is much harder than decluttering closets. Giving myself grace and sticking to the list of what's important was a challenge at first, but it has freed up so much time and energy that I can spend *with* my family now.

Boxing Day

It was December 26th that year, and I was happy. I had reclaimed my home, my holidays, and my purpose. I spent the day decluttering the house, putting away our gifts, and writing thank-you cards. Boxing Day may have started in the United Kingdom as a day to give gifts to household workers and tradespeople, but in the United States, the day after Christmas for me is a day to reset our home. The remnants from Christmas gift giving are easy to clean out. It's also easier to let go of some of the old toys or household items that have been replaced by new ones received as gifts. Before this year of transformation, I would have been scrambling to find places to put more stuff, but it was clearer to me and to my family that the peace we had achieved over the past several months was worth keeping. I wasn't as attached to the *things*, as I was to the feeling that I was in *control*.

The last week of the year, I went through my holiday Sunday Basket and consolidated my New Year and regular Sunday Baskets® back into one. The kids and I did a deep clean of each of their mini-apartments. Our home was not perfect and it never will be, but in all ways our life was more purposeful and more manageable. The holidays that year were really the icing on a very satisfying and magical cake that had taken since January to create.

With this year of transformation, I was even more ready to take on my future and to grow my Organize 365 business. I still do work my way through my home three times a year to keep the clutter at bay and to update my organizational systems as my life changes.

Year 2 & Beyond–Living an Organized Life

As I approach my 50th birthday, I am so grateful that my 39-year-old self had the courage to jump without a parachute, quit her job, and reclaim our home. I always knew that the only person I have control over is myself, and that eventful year, I lived it.

In the last decade there has been a running media theme that men are holding women back. I don't believe that. My husband, my father, and my son have all wholeheartedly supported all of my wildest dreams.

No, it's not men. I think it is our homes and our housekeeping expectations buried deep in our minds. Media and even personal memories have plagued women with promoting an unattainable, perfectionistic expectation of what our homes should look like and how they should function.

Function. Homes are meant to function for the people living inside them. Functional organizing isn't sexy. It doesn't sell magazines and will not cause Netflix to come knocking on my door for a TV special–but it *is* the answer.

A functionally organized home will build your confidence, reduce your anxiety, and give you buckets of time that you never realized you had. Then you will have a new problem.... what to do with all of that time!

At the end of my marathon organizing year, I had replaced my teaching salary. We were still deep in debt, but I knew that with consistent action, we would eventually overcome that obstacle, too.

I was a happier person, the mother I wanted to be, the wife Greg deserved, and the entrepreneur I always knew was my destiny. The last nine years have not been easy, but they have been *so* worth it. The woman I am today, who took responsibility for her life when everything was a mess, is the woman who can also take credit for the successes. You can, too!

We all want to achieve a beautiful, organized home today. The reality is that it took me a full year of focusing on my home to transform it. And, I think this is what is truly required. Decluttering and organizing each space in your home needs to be addressed in different seasons of the year and in different phases of life. A home that is "organized" is not static, but dynamic. You will need to put effort into adapting your home to best serve you as you grow and change. Continually evaluating your spaces and adapting will ensure you develop a comfortable maintenance rhythm that will sustain your new, organized life. And, when you reach a new phase of life or have an unexpected event, you will have the skills to reestablish your organized spaces.

Once you have learned the *skills* of organization, you will be ready for any of life's changes with the mental and physical skills necessary to move through the next transition with more peace and less anxiety. I cannot make the roller coaster of life not have its ups and downs, but your new organizational skills will make the ride more enjoyable.

Do you remember the start of this story? I was in crisis. You may be there now or know from recent experience exactly how that feels. So many women come to me in the middle of a crisis. They feel like failures, despite the fact that they have been juggling multiple jobs or roles for years. This is why I am so passionate about the transformation that comes with organizing, especially when I am able to share my particular experience. I really do "get it" and I really have changed my own life and the lives of countless others. This book is a testimony to my path, and you have likely seen yourself in more than one experience I've recounted. Change is possible, but mindset is everything! "Progress over perfection" can become your mantra, too. I invite you to join me! I'm honored to be a part of your transformational journey to a more peaceful, organized life.

Acknowledgements

In 2012, I knew I would start a company. Being a business owner has always been my dream. I watched my mother start a company from scratch in our basement, grow it to a presence in 24 states, and sell it–all during my grade school years. Then my father joined an established company, and worked his way into ownership. To one day own a company was always my dream. As I watched my parents, and reflected on how their parents were also business owners, I realized that I never aspired to work for someone. I aspired to create my own company.

Over the last decade, the Organize 365 blog I started in 2012 has transformed into a legitimate small business with 15 employees. In the last 3 years, I have reflected on and quoted the following quote from Bill Gates dozens of times, "Most people overestimate what they can achieve in a year and underestimate what they can achieve in ten years."

No doubt! Ten years ago, I had no idea that Organize 365 would manufacture and sell physical products from a warehouse with a fantastic full time staff. In 2012, I could never have imagined the team we have today in 2021. To be honest, I can hardly fathom what next year will look like, let alone 10 more years into the future.

In the year following the publishing of *The Paper Solution*, Organize 365 has added five more team members. While this book is my memoir, it would not exist without my amazing team and contractors who have helped us bring this story to life.

The editing team: Mary Nolan-Pleckham, Janet Harbort, and Kim Hueil worked together to take my raw story and added their editing genius for your reading enjoyment. Mary joined the Organize 365 team in 2017 and has been responsible for the written Organize 365 voice ever since. Mary's ability to translate my spoken podcast voice into a smooth reading experience is her super power. Janet was the original Organize 365 blog editor. I asked Janet to join us on this project, and I am so glad I did! Janet is responsible for creating the bonus journal prompts to support you as you embark on your own transformational year. And to my friend Kim, thank you for your detailed copy editing and eliminating all my ellipses...I use them in place of proper grammar.

The marketing team: Emily Kelly, Amy Proffitt, Michelle Paradice, Monique Horb, Emily Hare, and Shona Miklautsch. Thank you all for clarifying and amplifying the Organize 365 message. Your ability to think about our message as it relates to the website, social media, traditional media, Sunday Basket Certified Organizers, and customer service departments reduces audience anxiety and keeps our message empowering.

The operational team: Vanessa Nordmark, Pat Drybala, Sue Carey, Shari Banks, Joey Woodruff, Brayden Banks, and Stephanie Avalos. Thank you for sourcing, inventorying, and shipping the unique Organize 365 products that help our members implement their organizational systems. Here's hoping we can stay put until our lease is up!

That Bill Gates quote that I mentioned, "Most people overestimate what they can do in **one year** and underestimate what they can do in ten years." I'd like to rewrite it…

"Most people underestimate what taking a full 365 days to focus on getting organized will do to transform the next ten years of their lives."–Lisa Woodruff

Here's to your year of organizing. The world needs what you will create in the next ten years.

Take the Next Step in Your Organizational Journey.

O rganization is a learnable skill. You will be delighted at how your skills develop over time. You will never fully "get organized," because "organized" is not a static destination. Organization happens first in your mind, as you build an organizational mindset.

You can live a more organized life every day. Over time, you will learn what works best for your home, family, and life. Look for the functional solutions that work for *you* in this phase of life and for the family you have right now.

As you travel through each phase of life, how you use your space will change. You will need new organizational systems. It is an ongoing process. With each new phase of life, you will need to adjust your habits, routines, and systems, but you will already have the foundational skills of organization.

Organization involves constant pruning. The key is learning to let go of physical objects while retaining the memories associated with them. We are so blessed to be able to receive and give possessions freely. The more we give away, the more room for new memories to be made.

I don't often journal, but when I do, I am pleasantly surprised with what bubbles to the surface. I invite you to download the commentary journal prompts PDF at www.organize365.com/journalprompts. Spend some time in the next week thinking through your own organizational journey. You can also use this journal prompts PDF to facilitate a book study.

In the afterword, I have included information on the Sunday Basket® and the 100 Day Home Organization Program. The Sunday Basket® will eliminate your kitchen counter paper piles and keep all of your actionable papers organized. In the 100 Day Program, I will teach you the skills you need to have an organized home, and I have daily actionable steps that will get you there. I am here to cheer you on as you learn the organizational skills you need to transform your life and take back control of your home.

I look forward to helping *YOU* get organized!

The Sunday Basket®

The Complete Sunday Basket® System will help you to take back control of your home. You will get your kitchen counter paper, mail, and actionable to-do's organized. The Sunday Basket frees your mind from worrying if things will get done and allows you to focus your energy on what you *need* to get done. As you create the home organization habit of processing your Sunday Basket® each week, you will get five extra hours each week to spend doing what you are uniquely created to do.

I will give you the physical tools and the teaching you need to **learn the skills** of organization. I am a **functional** organizer so your final product will not be "Pinterest perfect"–though the Sunday Basket® *is* super cute! Functional organizing is my goal and I want to teach you how to get your paper organized! The Sunday Basket® is the **foundation** of all your organization and the launch pad of your transformation.

The Sunday Basket® comes with the Organize 365 custom designed Sunday Basket® container and 25 slash pockets to keep your paper organized. The Complete System also comes with training videos and a weekly online accountability and co-working group called the Sunday Basket® Club.

The Sunday Basket® will:

- Collect incoming paperwork
- Hold everything until you have time to process each item
- Help you to plan your week for maximum efficiency
- Keep your papers at your fingertips so you can easily take action on them
- Teach you the skills of organization for paper

The 100 Day Home Organization Program

The 100 Day Home Organization Program is a fast and detailed home organization program, designed to get your home organized in the most logical order without the organization being undone as you move from space to space.

Take the Organize 365 Productive CEO quiz online and pinpoint your "why" for getting organized, nail down how much time you can commit to getting organized, and discover where you are in the declutter/organize/productivity cycle. You can find the quiz for free at organize365.com/quiz

The 100 Day Home Organization Program is a collection of 100 daily actionable steps, along with videos and links to supporting podcasts and blog posts. The goal: to get your whole home organized in 100 days. Membership also includes access to a private Facebook group where you can find help and encouragement along your transformational journey.

The 100 Day Home Organization Challenge covers the main areas every homeowner needs to deal with:

- Kitchen and Food Organization
- Primary Bedroom, Bath, and Closet Organization
- Home Office, Books, and Electronic Organization
- Garage and Storage Room Organization
- Laundry Room and Cleaning Supply Organization
- Family Living Space Organization
- Home Maintenance Binder and Light Paper Organization

According to a Boston Marketing Firm, the average American wastes fifty-five minutes a day looking for things they own but can't find.[1] Spend the time up front and organize your home so that you do not spend it looking for things instead.

While I designed the challenge to be completed in as little as fifteen minutes a day, let's be honest. The real reason people want a fifteen-minute-a-day challenge is because they are overwhelmed, exhausted, and scared.

Overwhelmed at:

- the disorganized state of their home
- the energy it will take to do it all
- the idea of learning a different way of doing things

---

1   *Newsweek* (June 7, 2004)

Exhausted from:

- daily life
- looking for things and frustrated that they cannot find them
- living this way

Scared:

- that it works for everyone else, but it will not work for them
- that they will pay for the course, but not take the action
- that by committing to this challenge they have to change

What I have found is that the time limits fade once you see results.

Time and time again, our clients keep organizing when we leave their homes at night. And once you decide it is time to get organized, you are going to be staying up late and gleefully organizing on the weekends, too. I know it sounds crazy, but it is true. You will, because it is not about the amount of time you have.

Once you see that this works and you can do it, you will be empowered. You will start to look forward to making the decisions about where your stuff goes instead of living in the exhaustion and stress of your stuff telling you how to feel.

It is not all rosy.

As you can tell, I am an optimist. I am one of those "always happy even on rainy days" kind of people. But getting your whole home organized is hard, and it does take time to dig yourself out of the chaos.

Once you buy this membership, you have lifetime access. You can do the program as many times as you want. Your membership will never expire. You have access to all of the materials from the first day, and you can work at your own pace.

The first three to four weeks will be rough. Your inner voice will make up reasons why you lack the time, energy, or skills to do this, but you don't! And the mess will talk back to you, too. You will feel like you should be making more progress, faster.

But then it will happen. After Day 22, you will walk into your kitchen and it will be organized! And on Day 40, your primary bedroom, bath, closet, and accessories will all be completed as well. This will give you the power to move on to your books and office area.

I also want to give you a fair warning. Even though this is a 100 Day Program, I needed to do the program three times before my home felt really organized. I recommend that everyone plan to work through the program three times and allow a full year for your home to get fully organized. Decluttering during different seasons of the year helps you to see if you really *should* keep that turkey roasting pan and the camping tent. In the section on magazines, I teach you that most people can only declutter around 30 percent of their belongings at a time. Going back through the same parts of your home three times helps you to continue to analyze and get to the right amount of stuff for you.

So, if you are READY for a change, here is what the 100 Day Home Organization Program includes:

- 100 daily tasks that can be completed in as little as 15 minutes per day
- 100 daily videos to show you how to complete your tasks
- A goal setting planner with the daily tasks listed
- Planner training videos to help you get the most out of your planner
- Access to a private 100 Day Facebook group for community support

Sign up for your free trial week here: http://organize365.com/try-100/

Or, if you are ready to purchase, you can join today at https://organize365.com/100-Days/

I look forward to helping *you* get organized!

About the Author

Lisa Woodruff is a productivity specialist, home organization expert, and founder and CEO of Organize 365. Lisa provides physical and motivational resources teaching busy women to take back control of their lives with functional systems that work.

She's the host of the top-rated Organize 365 Podcast, which was featured as the Woman's Day podcast of the month. She shares strategies for reducing overwhelming thoughts, clearing mental clutter, and living a productive and organized life.

Lisa has authored several Amazon bestselling books and is a sought-after trainer and speaker, often quoted as saying "Done is better than perfect" and "Progress over perfection." Her sensible and doable organizing tasks appeal to multiple generations, and her candor and relatable style make you feel as though she is right there beside you, helping you get organized as you laugh and cry together.

As a recognized thought-leader, Lisa's work has been featured in many national publications such as The New York Times,

Fast Company, US News and World Report, Women's World, Ladies Home Journal, Getting Organized and Woman's Day magazines. She's been interviewed on over fifty podcasts, featured in more than fifty local TV segments, participated in countless online summits and is a regular HuffPost and ADDitude magazine contributor.

Lisa is also a generational expert and specializes in unpacking common everyday scenarios with grace, reshaping your understanding of the role we play in the home today. Believing that organization is not a skill you're born with, but rather one that is developed over time and which changes with each season of life, she made it her mission to redefine what it means to be a woman in the home.

Lisa lives in Cincinnati with her husband, Greg, and their children, Joey and Abby.

Made in the USA
Monee, IL
02 July 2021

72274134R00134